FIFTY GRADES OF HAY: THE COMPLETE TRILOGY

Derek the Weathersheep

DEDICATION

We'd like to dedicate this book to all our followers on Facebook and Twitter.

Although Derek the Weathersheep has his name on the front of the book, we'd would like to point out that this is Dolly's story, told in her own words.

We hope you enjoy it.

Derek and Dolly Weathersheep
Honey Farm
Brecon x

More books available at www.weathersheep.com

FIFTEEN GRADES OF HAY

1. A PARTY

I bleat with anger at my fleece. Damn my woolly locks. They just won't behave and damn Brenda for not letting me use her new fleece shampoo, especially the one formulated for flyaway fleeces.

Brenda is my barn-mate and has been for several years. A Cardiff girl, she's been around the block a bit. My best friend, she's the girl I can usually rely on. But today she's got the shits. Big time. One slight cough and the barn ain't going to smell too good.

The trouble is, is that she is supposed to be coming with me to the party in the farmhouse today. It is a sunny Easter Saturday afternoon. Farmer Honey and his wife are heading down to the market today so the girls do what they usually do when the house is empty and use the place for a knees-up. I guess I'm just going to have to go on my own.

"I'm sorry Dolly love. It's just my guts aren't feeling too good you know? They seem to be mulching over and over and I can't go sinking Rich Tea biscuits with the state I'm in. You'll be ok. The other girls are nice enough."

"I guess so." I say. "It's just that I've always been to parties with you in the past."

"Go on. Have a few biscuits for me eh? I'm just going to stay here in the barn with a cork up my arse."

I pop some lipstick on and head out across

the field to the farmhouse. By the time I get there, the party is already in full swing. I pass a girl on my way in, stood at the back door. She's part of Chain Command. She's there to alert us when Farmer Honey comes back.

There are two other girls – the first one is stood at the end of the field that overlooks the valley and the road leading up to the house. When she first sees Farmer Honey's Land Rover, she signals to one of the other girls, who is stood in the middle of the field. She then alerts the girl stood at the back door, who's already looking a bit worse for wear.

"You shouldn't be eating biscuits on duty." I say to her as I open the back door. She ignores me and I step inside. There are girls everywhere. Empty Hobnob packets litter the living room and biscuit barrels lie empty on the floor. I can hardly hear myself think above the sound of S Club 7 and I push my way towards the kitchen. I've never seen a party this wild. I just wish that Brenda was by my side. I'd feel a lot better if she was.

"Hobnob?" I get a chocolate biscuit shoved in my face.

"No thanks." I don't want to go straight for the hard stuff. "Got a Malted Milk?" A girl rummages around in a biscuit barrel.

"Nuh. All gone."

I head back into the living room. Maybe someone has left one lying round. I like Malted Milks. I like the pictures of the cows on them. They always feel a bit more substantial than say a Nice biscuit. There's a girl on her back in the middle of the floor. Legs in the air like she just don't care. There are two other girls kissing. One too many Digestives obviously. I'd never snogged a girl before and my eyes linger on them a little too long.

"What you looking at?" says the one girl, pulling away from the other.

"Just watching." I say. The girls carry on as if I'm not there.

Just then, there's a sudden thump at the back door. The door flies open and a few girls scream. I'm not sure what's going on exactly. Something's happening. Then the music stops. Everyone stops.

There is silence.

Then he speaks.

"Baaaaa!"

I'd never heard him speak before. In fact, I'd never seen him up close before. I'd only ever seen him sat on his own across the field. I'm captivated. I can't breathe. He is beautiful.

"Baaaa!" he shouts again. This time, there is a sudden reaction from the girls. And for me, the penny drops.

Farmer Honey is on his way home. And he's just a few minutes away.

2. A THANK YOU

The sudden wave of bodies heading for the door lifts me up off my feet. I'm literally being carried up and out of the house. Before I know it, I'm back outside in the field with all the other sheep. Farmer Honey's Land Rover pulls up outside. But I know that still in the house, is that good-looking boy. I'm worried for his safety.

***

It's a few hours later and I'm stood in the field talking with the girls.

"I'm going to have to say thank you." I say.

"For what?" says Tina.

"Raising the alarm and letting us know that Farmer Honey was on his way back. He probably got into a lot of trouble for that."

"I wouldn't bother. He didn't have to do it. I think he was just using it as an excuse to perv at us girls."

"I disagree." I say. "Who is he anyway?"

"Derek. Derek the Weathersheep. Bit of an odd one. Always sat over there in the field on his own. I've never spoken to him."

I gaze over at him sat there.

"He's a bit of a looker don't you think?" I say.

"He's alright I suppose."

I spend a few minutes plucking up the courage to go and speak to him. I decide to go. I trot off over the field. My legs are a little wobbly and my heart is all a-flutter. I keep telling myself to stay calm. As I approach, I noticed that his eyes are shut so I stop and stare.

I run my eyes down over his powerful frame. His limbs are sculpted, even at rest and sat there between his back legs are a sturdy set of large pink bollocks. He's all ram.

His eyes are closed and it's clear that he's pretending to be asleep.

"Don't pretend you're asleep." I say.

He sighs. Then he opens his eyes.

"I…we…we wanted to say thank you for what you did back there." I say. Then he goes off on one about how he's not a hero, and that it's something that anyone would have done in that situation and that although it'd be nice to appear on the Daily Mirror's 'Pride of Britain' Awards, he never really liked Piers Morgan, and in fact, he thinks Piers Morgan is a bit of an arsehole and should never have been given his own chat show after making so many people's lives a misery by hacking phones.

"Piers Morgan left the Mirror years ago. And it's never been proved in a court of law." I say.

"Yeah. Well. He's still a cock." says Derek.

I'm taken aback by his animosity toward Piers Morgan.

"Well I just wanted to say thank you." I say and with that, I turn and head back to the girls. My heart is still skipping. He actually spoke to me! I can feel his eyes burning into me as I walk away. And it's then that I realise that I'm moist downstairs.

***

I can't sleep that night. All I can do is think of Derek who is across the other side of the barn. Why don't any of the girls like him? Or were they just in denial? Do they not know that they had a demi-god in their midst? He is a handsome sheep. And not only that, he can forecast the weather.

Wow.

Later on in the day, I spot him stood high on the outcrop that looks out over the valley. He is obviously checking on the weather. What I like about him is that he is his own sheep. He doesn't need anyone to tell him what to do. He knows what he wants and he knows how to do it. I want to get to know him. As I stand there staring, he suddenly turns and our eyes meet.

Flummoxed, I pretend to half-wave and he nods back at me.

"What's the weather like today?" I shout.

"What?" comes his voice across the field.

"I said 'What's the weather like today?" I say.

"What?"

I sigh. "I said 'What's the weather like today?" I'm starting to feel stupid.

"What?"

'Jesus' I think to myself.

"Is it going to rain?"

"What?"

Ok, so this is getting a bit silly now. I can shout anything I want and he won't bloody hear me.

"Deaf bastard." I mutter under my breath.

"I'm not deaf." comes the reply.

***

Later on, I'm sat next to him and he's explaining the different cloud formations that hang in the sky.

"That one's a big rain cloud." he says but I'm not listening. My eyes are glued to his furry sheep arse. I just want to grab it and sink my teeth into it.

"And that one over there isn't a rain cloud. It's just a cloud."

"So Derek. Tell me about yourself." I say.

"What do you want to know?" he replies.

"Where you've come from. Why you don't talk to anyone else on the farm."

"I don't like other sheep." he says.

"Aw thanks." I say. It's a test.

"Nah, you're alright. The others – they just get on my tits."

"I know what you mean."

We sit there for a while without saying a word. My heart bulges at the thought that 'I'm alright'. We just sit there watching the day go by.

Derek finally breaks the silence.

"Do you fancy coming down to the trough with me?"

"Sure."

I've never been asked out for a drink together yet here I am with possibly the handsomest sheep in the field about to go to the trough.

"I haven't got any make-up on." I say.

"You don't need it. You're pretty enough as you are."

I blush.

"And besides you wear too much lipstick. You look like Zippo the Clown."

We get up together and begin our trot to the trough. He walks very closely beside me. I can almost feel the heat from his fleece. I look around. None of the other girls have noticed that I'm with HIM. Look at me girls. Here I am with Handsomesheep.com. Everyone look at me!

We arrive at the trough.

"You first." he says. I dunk my head into the trough. The cool water soothes my tingling lips. I know he's watching me. Then he speaks.

"Nice arse. Can I mount you some time?"

3. A KISS

"Derek the Weathersheep!" I exclaim. "How dare you!" I pretend to be offended. Inside, my body is crying out to be mounted by this king of sheep.

"I'm only asking." he says. "There's no harm in that is there?"

"I'm a woman. I have feelings and emotions. Aren't you going to try and woo me first? Maybe take me out down to the bottom of the field? I'd like to get to know you better first."

I am lying.

My head spins just at the thought of his masculine sheep shape bearing down on me.

"Oh ok. Just thought you might fancy it like." he says. "There's not much else going on around here."

"Well I'm not saying no. Just don't expect me to open my legs at the drop of a hat."

"Okay." he says and wanders off back up the field. I give chase. He keeps on walking.

"Are we okay?"

"What do you mean?" he asks.

"Me and you. We're okay aren't we?"

"Yeah, course. Why?"

"I just don't want you thinking I'm a slapper."

"You're not."

"Well that's a good thing isn't it?"

"Yeah." he says. His pace doesn't slacken.

"I'm off to check the weather if you don't mind." he says and heads off to the outcrop of rock in the distance. I stop and stand there in the middle of the field and sigh. I've blown my chance.

***

It's the very next day that I see him again. I'm busy eating some grass when I suddenly hear his voice behind me.

"What you doing?"

"Eating some grass."

I can sense him approaching from behind and it sends little pinpricks fizzing all over my body. I pretend not to notice. But I want it; I crave it.

'He has to be close' I say to myself. I wait. I wait for that first touch. But it doesn't come. Instead, he comes around to stand in front of me. He's looking gorgeous today. All wool and muscle. I can't stop my stomach doing somersaults.

"Want to come and see my weather charts?" he asks.

"What for?"

"You said you wanted to get to know me better."

"Okay" I say.

We head to the place where Derek likes to sit. The grass is already flattened and I sit down next to a pile of papers.

Over the next hour or so, I pretend to listen and take an interest but it all goes over my head. I can't take my eyes off his lipstick that keeps popping out and it's only a matter of time before he catches me looking.

"You looking at my sausage?"

I blush. I can do nothing but giggle. "Well it is sat there winking at me."

"Pervert." he says before pulling out another chart. I'm still smiling.

"Here. Take a look at this. It's an isobar chart. These wiggly lines here….." His voice drifts away as I lose myself in my thoughts – a heady concoction of lust and wool.

Before I know it, this Adonis of sheep is stood right in front of me. He's looking right at me with those beautiful yellow eyes and his woolly chest is puffed out.

He moves closer.

"What are you doing?" My voice cracks and he moves closer again. My heart is thumping against my ribcage, desperate to get out. My throat tightens. My legs tremble. He is inches from my face. I can smell his musky sheep smell. It fills my nostrils.

And then he kisses me.

His sheep lips, so soft, connect with mine. I close my eyes and my mind goes into a spin. I don't know where I am. But it's heavenly. And then he pulls away. My eyes are still closed but I can feel a huge smile ripple across my face.

"You brushed your teeth this morning?" he says "You smell like a Biffa."

***

When I get back to the girls, I'm bursting to tell them. I decide not to though. I decide that I'd like to have that dirty secret in my head. When all the other girls complain about being single, I can congratulate myself on having kissed the handsomest sheep on the farm.

"What you been up to over there?" says Tina.

"Oh Derek's been showing me some weather charts."

"He's a boring git isn't he?"

"I don't think so. He's different to a lot of sheep. And he's very talented."

"Each to their own. You got any plans for the weekend? There's a new series of Take Me Out starting this Saturday."

I hadn't thought that far ahead. All I am thinking of is Derek and that kiss. It's what I think about for the next few hours and every now and then, I slip back to that moment.

The following day, I'm back with Derek.

He's playing things pretty cool but inside, I'm all chewed up. I try to think up some weather-related comment.

"It hasn't rained for ages has it?"

"Seven weeks and four days now. But that's about to change. I can feel it. My charts also show a ridge of low pressure moving up from the continent which will bring some summery showers." I quiver at his mastery of all things meteorological. This man is the whole package.

Far away, over at the farm house, Farmer Honey is climbing up a ladder with a pot of paint. Round the side of the house, Mrs Honey is busy pegging out some washing on the line.

"Hm. I don't think that's a very good idea." says Derek. "He obviously hasn't checked his grazier's weather report. I'll need to let him know."

Derek rises up and heads off over the field to the house. I watch as he starts getting the attention of Farmer Honey. Derek then drags him across the field to the outcrop to show him the dark clouds gathering behind the mountains. A few seconds later, Farmer Honey is running back to the house, shouting out for Mrs Honey to get her smalls back in off the washing line.

Derek has saved the day. My hero.

He trots back to where I am sitting beaming with pride. My man. I'm very proud of him.

"We'd best head indoors. The rain isn't too far off."

We head into the barn and Derek invites me over to his patch. We settle down and it's not long before the rain starts thundering down on the roof of the barn. Surprisingly, the rest of the flock are still outside.

"They're under the old oak tree." says Derek. "It's just me and you."

My heart starts thumping. And Derek moves closer. He gently pushes me on my back and moves in to kiss me again. I can hardly breathe. Taking charge, he moves a hoof up over one of my legs. I try to speak but he simply puts a hoof on my mouth.

"Shhh…" he says and then presses his lips onto mine. The kiss is electric and I can't help myself. I grab the back of his head and lose myself in him.

He presses himself hard against me. I can feel his chipolata, now pumping up to the size of a small Greggs sausage roll, rubbing up against me.

"I want you." I say.

"I know." he says, grabbing my head and forcing it back. He's kissing my neck and I feel totally at his mercy. I'm exposed but it's thrilling me. I hadn't felt this good since Shakin' Stevens returned to the charts in 2005.

He bears his weight down on me and I open my legs for him. He's grinding his hips into mine, and I thrust myself upward to meet him.

"I want to shag you," he says "I want to shag you like a sheep."

"I want you to shag me." I say, but I can hardly get the words out. I'm longing for him to have me, to take me.

"Just stick it in!" I call out. He ignores me. He teases me. His bangstick is throbbing and I reach out to grab it. It's hot.

"Stick it in me." I growl. I want him inside me now. I want him bad. But he still ignores me. It's driving me wild.

Just then, there's a long creak as the barn door slowly opens. The sound of the rain outside suddenly splashes into the barn.

"Someone's there!" I say.

"I know." says Derek, pinning me down. "That's what I was hoping for."

4. AN ARRIVAL

I'm walking on air for the following week. Derek is playing it cool as he always does and our encounter is never mentioned. Not by him anyway.

"What's the weather going to do today Dolly?" asks Tina in a sarcastic tone.

"I don't actually know." I say.

"Well you spend most of the day with the so-called weather expert. You're hardly over here with us anymore."

"Jealous are we?" I ask.

"No. Not at all." says Tina. "Will you be watching Take Me Out with HIM this weekend?"

"I'm not sure. I'll let you know." I reply and trot off to get some time away from her.

It's as I'm walking across the field that a roar of a lorry shatters the peace. The lorry pulls up outside the farm and a tall guy gets out and knocks on the farm house door. I sit down on the grass to watch what's going on. I can see Derek watching from his place on the outcrop.

Farmer Honey comes to the door and both him and the tall guy walk around the back of the lorry. Looks like we've got a new arrival.

Off the back of the lorry comes this sheep. He's VERY handsome and stands there surveying the area like he owns the place. I'm not sure if it was because of my encounter with Derek the other day, but this sheep is giving me a throb-on. He's giving me a tingle in my dingle. God, what's happening to me? I'm becoming a bit of a nymph.

I look over to Derek. He's now sat bolt upright. He's been watching me watching this new guy. Bit of jealousy going on there?

I'm introduced to the new boy a little later in the day. He's sat talking to Tina.

"This is Dolly." she says. He casts me a glance before holding my gaze.

"And who are you?" I ask.

"His name's Juan and he's from Spain. He doesn't speak much English." says Tina on his behalf.

"I only speak da language of love." he pipes up.

"I see." I say and head on over to see Derek. Derek isn't happy.

"Who's the new guy?" he asks.

"Some Spanish guy. Speaks the language of love apparently."

"Tosser." says Derek lifting up a chart and patting it out on the grass.

∗∗∗

"It's not what it seems." says Juan in his clipped Spanish tones. I look up. I'm on the floor outside the barn, it's dark and Juan is stood over me. What is going on? Last thing I knew I was asleep inside.

"Yeah? Well go ahead. Explain away!" It's Derek's voice and he's not happy. I've got no idea what's going on.

"Well…" stutters Juan, "It's like this…erm… I've got a bolus up my arse and I was asking Dolly to take it out for me." His English clearly isn't that bad.

"A bolus? What the hell is a bolus?"

bellows Derek.

"Medicine. It's up my arse."

"Is it supposed to be up there?"

"Yes. But I don't want it up there. It affects my confidence as a man."

I have to get to my feet. My heads hurts and I'm confused.

"What's going on?" I ask.

"Get over here behind me Dolly." Derek snaps. I make my way into the barn and lie back where I had been lying the last time I was awake. I can hear Derek laying down the law to Juan outside the barn and a few minutes later, he comes back in and cwtches up next to me.

"What was that all about? Why was I outside?" I ask.

"You don't want to know."

"I'd like to know seeing as I there!" I retort.

"He had his big Spanish bollocks in your face."

I don't know whether to laugh or cry. Juan was a nice-looking specimen, don't get me wrong, but if he was going to put his bollocks in my face, it would have been nice to have been asked beforehand.

"How did I get outside the barn?"

"God knows. Come on. Get some sleep."

Derek closes his eyes and lets out a deep sigh. Secretly, I'm slightly gutted that I was asleep during all of this. I wouldn't utter a word of this to Derek of course.

I wake up a few hours later. Derek is still behind me but all the other girls are out in the field.

"You awake?" I ask.

"Yes."

"How come you're not on Facebook

updating the weather forecasts?"

"I'm happy here." He moves in closer behind me. I can sense he's feeling fruity. Sure enough, a few moments later, I feel his lipstick poking me in the back.

"Wanting some more are you Mr Derek?" He just lets out a groan, and grabs my hip, forcing himself closer to me. I'm ready for him to take me but there's a sudden creak as the barn door opens and in steps Juan. He looks over to where Derek and I are lying.

Without warning, Derek forces himself inside me, forcing me to squeal. He knows that Juan is watching. He's marking his territory. Derek moves his love truncheon inside me but my gaze is still fixed on Juan who stands there watching. I'm being had by one handsome sheep and I'm being watched by another. The exhilaration becomes too much and waves of lust ripple throughout my body. I want more. I push back on Derek. I want to be had. I want to be had hard. I want to be had hard by Derek the Weathersheep and I want Juan to watch.

I can't stop myself. I close my eyes as a tsunami of warm fizz rises up and spreads out from my foofer across my entire body. I'm helpless. Behind me, Derek grunts his way to his climax before letting out a big sigh.

I open my eyes. Juan has gone, leaving the barn door wide open.

"Anyone would think he was born in a barn." says Derek.

"He probably was." I say.

5. A JUMP

Derek is stood on a bale of hay in the middle of the barn.

"Girls, girls, GIRLS!" he shouts.

The murmuring soon drops to a hush while we wait for Derek to speak.

"I'd first like to thank you for coming along today." he says. "Now…as you all know, it's the Royal Welsh Show coming up in a few weeks' time. And as we all know, they do the same thing year in year out. A few cows walk around a ring and a few dogs chase sheep. I thought it was time for change. Real change. Time for us sheep to really show what we are made of. What I propose is that we put on a sky dive."

There is a bit of a commotion among the girls.

"A sky dive?" someone calls out. "How the hell are we going to do that? We've got no parachutes and no aeroplane."

"Ah. But that's where you're wrong," says Derek "We have parachutes AND we have an aeroplane."

There is another commotion among the small crowd.

"But what's the point?" someone calls out.

"Because we can." replies Derek.

There is a collective groan and the girls then troupe out of the barn. There are a few mumbles of 'dickhead' and 'arsehole' as they pile out. I am the only one that's left.

"I believe in you Derek the Weathersheep." I say, looking up at him.

It is unusual for a sheep to want to do a sky-dive. But that's what I admire about Derek. He's a leader. A leader among sheep. But I can't stop thinking about Juan.

***

"I want you to be my girlfriend. Properly." says Derek.

"What do you mean?"

"Like a proper boyfriend and girlfriend. So that we buy each other Valentine's Day cards and stuff like that."

"No. I mean why do you want me to be your girlfriend?"

"You've got a nice set of teets and I don't fancy any other the other girls on the farm."

I'm not sure what Derek is up to. Why would he want to make things official? Is it because of the arrival of Juan?

"I'm not sure that I want to get too formal about things." I say. And I mean it. Being a girlfriend involves doing things like cleaning and going to Kwik Save and stuff.

"Why not?" I can tell Derek is put out.

"We can go for walks down to the bottom of the field together and stuff."

"We do that anyway." I reply.

"Well we can make love instead of just bonking."

"Make love?" It's a phrase I've come to detest over the years.

"Make love? How can you 'make love'?"

"Easy. Just stick it in, tell each other that you love each other. Erm… and that's it."

says Derek. I look out over the fields. I'm not sure I want a full-time boyfriend. I'd quite like to have a go at Juan if I can. Keep my options open. Derek's lovely and all that but he has turned out a bit boring. From what I know about Juan, he seems more mercurial.

"I'll think about it." I say.

Derek sighs. "What is there to think about?" he asks.

"Don't pressurise me." I say.

"I'm doing this sky-dive for you." he says.

"What do you mean?"

"To prove I'm not boring." Has he been reading my mind? What else does he know?

"Look. I think you're lovely and all that, I really do. I just don't want to rush into things in case it goes wrong and we end up losing our friendship."

"Can we still shag?"

"Yeah course."

"Lovely. That'll do." Derek rises to his feet. "Excellent. Right. I'm off for a dump."

He trots off down the field and leaves me wondering. What am I doing? First, I get jiggy with Derek and now someone better-looking comes along.

Can't I have both? Sometimes, you should be careful what you wish for.

6. JEALOUSY

Derek does his jump and if I'm totally honest, it does make me feel more attracted to him. For a sheep to go up in a plane and jump out and land on all four feet (even if he was 3 miles off course) makes me think that he's a special sheep.

I treat him to some action later as a reward. For a few weeks, things are good between Derek and I. It does almost feel that we are boyfriend and girlfriend and Juan keeps his distance, leaving me to forget him a little.

But one sunny afternoon, when I'm sat in the field on my own soaking up the sun's rays, Tina comes waddling over. She's walking like John Wayne would if he was a sheep.

"What's up with you?" I ask. Tina plops down next to me.

"Just had a good seeing to from Juan behind the barn." she says.

That searing heat of jealousy rises up within me.

"He gave it to me good and proper."

"You mean you had intercourse?" I ask.

"Intercourse? Are you some kind of sex education teacher? No-one calls it that any more. But yes, there was full penetration of Juan's penis into my pelvic cavity if that's what you're asking."

"Well how did that come about?"

"He just asked if I fancied it and I said yes and off we went."

"Just like that?"

"Yes, just like that. You need to get out more Dolly love."

Tina lays back, clearly struggling with the pounding she'd taken from Juan. I feel sick. Tina's gone and tasted Juan's beef bazooka when it was all I had been thinking about up until a few weeks ago.

How dare she.

"He's a big lad." says Tina.

"I don't want to know." I reply. I do, but I don't.

Tina continues. "It looked and felt like a Saturn V. There it was, sat on the launch pad. I couldn't help but sit on it. And then came the same turbulent thrusting force and energy that can send a man to the moon. Fair play to the lad. Just as a rocket can send a satellite into orbit, he sent me into orgasm, which is no less awesome a feat."

I don't want to hear any more. I want to go find him to see what the idiot was playing at. I get up and leave Tina to her sore bits.

"Where you going?" she shouts.

"Back in a minute."

***

I find Juan relaxing at the top of the field. His eyes are closed and he has a slight smirk on his face.

"Hello Dolly." he says without opening his eyes.

"How do you know it's me?"

"I knew you'd come once Tina told you."

I'm angry. What an arrogant arsehole.

"Jealous aren't you?" I hate him. I hate his stupid accent and I hate his stupid everything. I spin around and head back off down the field.

Behind me, I hear Juan chuckling to himself.

As evening falls, Derek comes down from his rock outcrop and comes over to me. I'm sitting alone in the field. And I'm not in a good mood.

"What's the matter?" asks Derek.

"I'm fine. Nothing." He sits next to me.

"What is it?"

"Nothing. I'm fine." I've got so much anger inside me but it's not Derek's fault. I turn to him and smile.

"Shall we head to the barn? The other sheep are still out in the field." Derek's face lights up.

"Excellent." he says. I'll just swill my schlong in the sheepdip. Meet you in there."

When I get to the barn, my friend Brenda's lying there next to where I would usually lie.

"You ok?" I ask.

"Yeah. Just came in for a lie down.

t's too hot out there."

I lie down next to her. We both look up at the ceiling of the barn.

"What brings you in here then?" asks Brenda. Just then, Derek arrives at the barn door. He looks surprised to see me there with Brenda.

"Ahhh." says Brenda. "I get it. Well don't let me stop you two. I'm not moving."

A smile wraps around Derek's face and he comes to lie down next to me.

"We can't do anything with Brenda here." I say.

"Why not?"

"Ah get on with it. I've seen it all before." says Brenda. I feel Derek run his hoof over my foof. It sends a tingle shooting up to my belly. I'm so wanting some action but I feel a little bit self-conscious with Brenda lying next to me. Derek presses his big sheep lips down onto mine.

I submit.

I wrap my front leg around the back of Derek's head and draw him in closer. He's making me tremble so much that it's registering on the Dichter Scale. His hooves are all over my lactoids.

"Kiss my butterbags." I wail. He grabs them.

"Great set of Zepplins." he says, sliding his hoof down between my legs and over my Volvo. I reach out to grab his jigger, but he holds me down and slides his woolly face down between my legs. Within seconds, he's performing tongue fu on my Beetle bonnet.

To my surprise, I feel another hoof touching my pontoons.

"Sorry." says Brenda. "I couldn't resist." I gasp as two pairs of hooves slide over my body. I'm shaking like a shitting dog. The only thing I wish for was that Juan could be here.

"Take me Derek." I cry out.

"Yes, take her." says Brenda. Derek moves back up, his clockweights dangling between his legs. His panhandle looks glorious. Even Brenda looks on with awe.

"Didn't know you were amphibious." says Derek to Brenda.

"I do like to growl at the badger every now and then yes." she replies. "Half chips, half rice me."

I moan in ecstasy as Derek bears his weight down on me. And I'm so ready for him, it's a hole in one.

***

We're still lying there when the rest of the flock come back into the barn for the evening. Juan looks over and sees us red-faced. I smile at him and he smiles back.

"Do you fancy him?" asks Derek. He's obviously clocked us exchanging smiles.

"I don't fancy him. I think he's goodlooking but I don't fancy him." I reply.

"Birrova ladies man that one, Billy Big Bollocks." says Brenda." I wouldn't go there though."

It's during the early hours of the morning when Dai the Llama burst into the barn. His night-vision goggles scan the barn.

"Everyone ok?" he says.

There are a few grumbles. From the corner of the barn comes the sound of a strangled fart.

"No riots in here then?"

No-one answers. There are a few more groans and then Dai closes the door and went back out to patrol the field.

We find out the next day that there are riots all around the country. We get a pair of goat twins to look after the farm. They're pretty hot and the rest of the girls pay them a lot of attention. But my head is already full.

I'm torn. I'm going with Derek but wanting to go with Juan. Our romantic interlude with Brenda has opened my eyes to the possibility of all sorts of possibilities. Yet the two guys don't like each other much. My ultimate fantasy of being in the middle of a ram sandwich seems like a very remote possibility.

I need to sort my head out. Make a commitment. I needed to get Juan out of my mind for good. The was the plan at least until he came into the barn one day while I was alone.

7. A MONSTER

"How's your clackervalve?" Juan has entered the barn when I am alone.

"Fine thank you. How was Tina's?" I reply.

"Very good thank you." He sits next to me.

"So. When can I park my pink bus in your furry garage?"

"That ain't going to happen."

"Well I can't sit around doing the Palma Sutra for the rest of my days."

"You got Tina." I say.

"Tina? You think I'll be going back there again? I don't think so."

"I'm not interested thank you."

"You're not interested in my wife-tamer?" he says. I turn to see him and am shocked to see him sat there with his stoat in his hands. It is impressive and my jaw drops.

"Don't tell me you aren't interested in this?"

I need to get away. He has had his chance but I need to get away. If not for my sake, for Derek's. But I can't take my eyes off Juan's tool. It's huge. It looks rock solid. So much so that there appears to be a miniature double of myself on it shiny head. A doppleganger dick.

"Put it away." I say but secretly, I want it. The roar of Farmer Honey's tractor pulling up outside disturbs us and Juan swiftly moves to the far side of the barn with his five legs. My face is still glowing. I can see why Tina couldn't resist. I head outside to get some fresh air.

Derek is with Dai Llama, talking tactics about how they are going to patrol the farm at night. Hoodies need to be kept away.

"You'll be on your own tonight." says Derek. "I'll be out here with Dai patrolling the field. At least you'll have Brenda to keep you company." he says and winks.

Brenda did keep me company. We had a bit of a fun while Derek was away. I couldn't stop myself. And by morning, I was still tingling. Which was awkward when Juan turned up at the trough.

"This water is horrible." he says. "Giving me stomach cramps."

"I guess you're used to Spanish water huh?"

"Yes. Over there, the water is crystal clear. This stuff is murky." he says.

"Well it's all you're going to get around here."

"What have you been up to ?" he asks. All I can think about is that image of his standing ovation.

"Nothing much. You?"

"This and that. Romancing the bone last night."

"Yeah? How is Tina?"

"Don't know." he replies. "She wasn't there." I turn to him.

"Who was the lucky girl last night then?"

"I forget her name." His negative psychology is working. He knows what he's doing. My groins throb. I want him more than ever. Everyone else is getting a piece of that meat. I wanted to experience it.

***

It feels odd snuggling up to Derek that night. I feel comfortable around Derek and I feel that I do love him. But Juan is such a bad sheep.

"What you thinking about?" Derek asks as he cwtches me from behind.

"Just stuff."

"Oh. Good stuff I hope."

"Yea. All good ta."

As I drift off to sleep, all I can think about is Juan.

★

'It's not right' I think to myself. This shouldn't be happening. Why am I wasting so much time thinking about Juan when I have a perfectly delicious man in Derek? I feel I need to clear the air. I also think that Derek should know what's going on. If I can't be totally honest with him, then there's no point us being together.

I head up to see Derek in the field. It's another gloriously hot day but I'm nervous. How will Derek react when I tell him about my feelings for Juan?

Derek is on his new laptop, updating his friends on Facebook. He notices me arriving and looks up.

"Hiya love. You ok?"

"Yeah. Sort of. We need to talk."

"About what? You sure you're ok?"

I sit down next to him. He looks worried.

"I want you to know firstly that I like you. Really, really like you. And I think that I'm falling for you."

Derek smiles. Such a lovely sheepy smile. How can I hurt him? But he needs to know. I take a big breath.

"It's Juan. I think I'm in love with him too."

8. A PROPOSAL

"So you want to go with him too or instead of me?"

"It's not like that."

"It's exactly like that from where I'm sitting." I sigh. "I'm just being honest with you. I do really, really like you. I guess it's more of an infatuation with him. All the girls seem to be getting in on the act and I just feel that I'm missing out."

Derek falls silent. I feel awful. I move towards him to give him a kiss but he reels away.

"I guess there's no point in carrying on this conversation." I say and get up to walk away.

"Sit down." says Derek. I sit back down.

"Look. There's something I've been meaning to tell you too." I'm confused.

Derek packs away his laptop and holds my hooves in his. He thinks hard before he speaks.

"If we're being totally honest about things, then I need to come clean too."

"Go on." I say.

"It's Brenda."

"What about her?" I ask. I feel a sudden rage building up within me.

"A few nights ago…when you were asleep… after that group thing we did…."

"What? What happened?"

"I'm sorry. I thought it was you."

"What did you do?"

"I was half asleep and she was there in front of me."

"You poked her?"

"Well not quite. I wasn't fully recovered from our session. I wasn't as hard as I would have liked. It was like playing snooker with a piece of string."

I wait for more.

"Eventually I managed to get it in but it was like packing a marshmallow in there. I thought it was you."

I'm shocked.

"I'm sorry." says Derek. I don't know what to say. I've gone from feeling like a bitch to feeling like a woman scorned.

"Well what do we do from here?" I ask.

"If you want to make things equal, then you can go with Juan. If that makes you feel better." It's an offer only a few moments ago that I would have jumped at. But suddenly, it all seems irrelevant.

"Ok. Fine." I say. "I will." I stand up and trot off. I'm not sure if I mean it but I want Derek to feel some of my pain. As fate would have it, the first person I bump into is Juan as he heads out into the field.

His tackle swings between his hind legs like a large bag of giblets.

"Hey. Spanish boy. You want to go with me?" I say, throwing all caution to the wind.

"Sure." he says. "When?"

"Tonight. Meet me at the top of the field."

"Lovely." he says.

✳✳✳

I'm nervous as I head out to the field that night. I glance at Derek who is sitting down with Brenda in the barn. I harbour no ill feelings towards her. I did enjoy playing her gusset piano.

The field is dark but I can make out Juan's outline against the night sky. It's a cool evening and I wonder how hot things are going to be.

I look back at the barn and think of Derek. But then I picture him with his lipstick inside Brenda while I lie sleeping next to him. And I march on harder up the field.

"Good evening." he says as I approach him. I can't see him clearly but he's sat in the same position I found him in the barn that day. He was ready for me.

9. A RAM SANDWICH

We don't speak. We get straight to it. No time for choreplay. His parson's sack feels swollen. He's obviously been saving himself for me.

He's working my underbeard with his hooves in advance of serving his main course. I can't wait and get my head down between his legs. I go at his bell tower like a woodpecker. And he's big. He's got the girth of a National Express coach and the length of a Thames barge. No wonder Tina was walking like John Wayne.

He begins talking in Spanish. Such a turn on. But I'm needing to get him inside me and quick. He picks me up, throws me over a nearby hay bale and drills his spam javelin inside me. I feel like I'm being torn in two.

He grabs me by the back of the head and lifts it up.

"Looks like we've got company." he says.

I peer into the darkness. I can't see anything. I try to speak but I'm having all the air in my lungs banged out of me.

"And it looks like it's your man." I look again.

Sure enough, looming out of the darkness is Derek.

"Come to watch?" calls Juan. I hear Derek's voice call back.

"No. I've come to join in." The thought sends me wild. Before I know it, Derek is stood right in front of me. His soldier of love is just inches from my mouth.

"You're very welcome." says Juan. I get little say in the matter. I can hardly speak.

"To me." says Derek.

"To you." replies Juan.

"Let Percy in the playpen." I'm beginning to lose all sense of everything. All I know is, is that I'm being taken from both ends by the Chuckle Brothers. And I'm loving it.

They swap ends. I hardly get a moment to breathe before Juan opens my mouth and fills it with his thunder-rod.

But then it all goes horribly wrong. Derek is going at me from behind like the clappers. But Juan pulls out.

"I'm sorry." he says. "I've got a grumbling stomach. It must be the water round here. It's making me ill."

With that, he holds his stomach and lets out a shot gun fart which peppers pellets of crapnel into a small pile on the floor by his hooves.

"I'm sorry, I'm so sorry." he says. He clutches his stomach again and now floats an air biscuit right into my face.

I feel sick. Juan runs off down the field, clutching his stomach and still parping.

"Well." says Derek. "Shall I finish you off?"

"Yes please." I say.

10. MY MAN

The next day, Juan keeps himself to himself. Every time I see him, I get a warm waft of sheep shit in my nostrils. Derek is back in the field, checking his charts. I head over to him.

"Are we even Stevens now?" I say, taking my place next to him.

"Aye. I guess so." he says. "You know, I know that you love me and I also know that there are other good-looking men out there. I can't compete with all of them. As long as I'm the one you love, I don't mind you looking."

"Aw. And do you mind me going with them?" I say.

"As long as we're all in the same room." he replies. "I'd feel a bit greedy keeping you all to myself."

I sit back and look over the fields. The sun is scorching the fields in the valley below but a cool breeze flutters over us.

"We're going to have a great summer aren't we Derek the Weathersheep?" I say.

"Yes Dolly. We are."

FIFTEEN GRADES OF HAY: THE SEX TAPE

1. A HEADACHE

"I've got a headache." I say.

"Again?"

"Yes."

"But you get a headache every time I come close to you." says Derek.

"I'm just not in the mood for it this morning. Now please move those stonads away."

"Stonads?"

"Move it!" I snap.

"But you promised..."

"The crimson tide is in." I say. It's a lie.

"The tomato boat has docked again has it? Jeez. You have the painters in more times than the Forth Bridge."

Derek moves away, sighing. It was only a matter of months ago that Derek was tromboning me hard every morning. These days, I'd rather he didn't try grinding his middle stump into my back every time I wake up. I have more important things to do. Like sleep. Or just lying there doing nothing whatsoever.

"I'm going out to check the weather." he says, getting up and heading outside. I stretch out star-shaped in the hay and drift back to sleep.

***

It's a good few hours later when I wake. It's a grim,

grey rainy day. Most of the ewes on the farm are stuck in the barn. None of them want to venture outside. My bestie, Brenda, is lying next to me.

"You two getting on alright?" she asks, noticing that I'm finally awake.

"Yeah, we're good thanks."

Brenda's eyes linger on me. It's then that I notice that Derek is still outside in the rain.

"Where's Derek?" I ask.

"Outside. He's been out there for hours." she replies. I struggle wearily to my hooves and move over to the barn door and look out. Veils of rain drag themselves across the sodden field. In the far grey stands Derek. He spots me looking out at him, then turns away and continues to look out into the fog. What has happened to us? We've gone from the horniest celebrity sheep couple in Wales to a pair of frigid old decrepits in a matter of months.

Derek finally returns to the barn another two hours later. He's dripping wet. Brenda puts her head back down and pretends that she's asleep. She witnesses the same routine every evening.

"Where you been?" I ask.

"Out watching the weather."

"It's raining. Even I could have told you that." I reply.

"What's on telly tonight?"

"Erm…Corrie…Eastenders. Then there's a new show on about a detective trying to solve some murders. It's supposed to be quite good."

"Hm. Don't fancy that. I'll probably go and work on some weather charts." he says, and trots over to the far side of the barn. I sigh. It's the same thing every day – woken by Derek's bangstick being shoved in my back, I pretend I've got a headache, he goes outside for the day and then if I'm lucky, he'll come back in and spend some quality time watching telly with me later on in the evening. Then we go to sleep. It's not what I signed up for.

"Have you seen the new boy?" asks Brenda.

"Is this the one from Berkshire? I've heard he's a bit of a looker." I say.

"Yeah, he's not bad. Not as slimy as Juan and a bit of a toff. But I'd still consider siphoning his python."

I gasp. "That's not like you Brend. You're usually very fussy about who you'd play Hide the Salami with."

"Well he gave me a throb-on when I first saw him. Maybe it's my age. Maybe I'm getting desperate. There he is now."

Strutting in out of the rain he comes, like some sort of woolly Adonis. A murmur ripples throughout the barn as he walks amongst the girls, all eyes fixed on his masculine frame. And by God he knows it.

"Good Lord." I say, my pudding instantly throbbing like a Belisha Beacon.

"Yep. Thought you might say that." says Brenda.

"Wow. He'll be in my thoughts when I'm gusset-typing later on." I say.

Our eyes watch him as he takes his place in the hay. He stands, proudly surveying the barn before lowering himself to the hay and stretching out.

"Do you think he's all there downstairs?" I ask.

"Hung like a walrus apparently." replies Brenda.

"Hm. I'd like to find out." I say.

"What about Derek?" asks Brenda.

"What the eyes don't see, the heart doesn't grieve." I reply.

"Now be careful Doll. Look what happened with Juan the Lovesheep."

I manage to catch myself.

"Yes. You're right. Of course. I shouldn't even think of going there." I say, relaxing back in the hay.

I lie again. I want him.

2. A PROPOSAL

The following morning is a sunny one. Derek is off down the far end of the field and I'm still indoors. The morning 'headache' ritual is now several hours behind us. Then, without warning, the god-like form of Tarquin struts into the barn like some kind of peacock and makes a beeline straight for me. My heart leaps. He arrives and looks me up and down.

"Where's the hubster? Orf doing one's weather?" he says, nose in the air. He seems very acquainted with me yet we've never spoken. He moves on over and takes a seat next to me.

"Hello." I say. "I'm Dolly. Pleased to meet you." My eyes wander over the chiseled features of his rugged face.

"On your own?"

"Yes." I sense he's wanting something.

"You look like a lovely girl. Top drawer, you know what I mean? But I've seen you with that Weatherboy. You don't look happy you know. Something's missing."

"Derek and I are fine, thank you."

"You know what? You need someone more like me in your life. More adventurous, more open-minded, more masculine. You'd enjoy your time with me for instance. I sleep in a tent, if you know what I mean." he says, leaning into me. I'm taken aback by his forthright words. How can he know me so well? We've only just met.

"As I say, Derek and I are doing just fine thank you. Why is everyone asking if we're ok?" I say.

"I bet he was there rubbing his kipper all over your back this morning. And I bet that you told him you had a headache because you weren't interested. And I bet that he had to go away and let off several rounds of his mutton musket on his own in the corner of the field. I've seen it all before. It's called a relationship."

"And what would you know about relationships?" I say, slightly vexed at his arrogance.

"I know not to go anywhere near them. They ruin your sex life. You need an affair, that's what you need. Something to excite you. Does Derek ever tie you up? Does he ever film you?"

"That's none of your business."

"That's a no then. Do you know what I got up to just before I came to this poxy little Welsh farm? You see, I'm into S&M. Those girls on that farm knew how to show a handsome cad like me a jolly good time. They tied me up like some ruddy great Christmas turkey and then took it in turns to ride me."

I pretend I'm not interested. But I am. I want to hear more.

"I'm not interested."

He continues. "And do you know what the best bit of all was? They filmed it for me and handed it to me on VHS for me to watch afterwards. Now that's what I call real women." he says.

His words anger yet excite me. Why is he telling me all this? I've only just met him. Yet I'm jealous. I want that kind of excitement in my life. I hadn't felt excitement since my dabblings with Juan the Lovesheep. Spanish Boy keeps his nose out of things these days.

In a perverse way, it's nice to have another sheep paying me some attention. I feel a stirring in my groins. And he knows it.

"So how about it Dolly bird?" he says.

"Right here. Right now. Weatherboy'll never know."

"How about what?" I ask. I want to hear what he's got to offer.

"Me and you having a bit of rumpo. I've always fancied porking a Valleys girl after seeing how easy they were on that MTV show."

"You're a right charmer aren't you?" I say.

"Never had anyone refuse me." he says.

Despite his arrogance, I feel drawn to him. Like a fly to a freshly laid turd on a summer's day. I get a tingle in my dingle and I come over all unnecessary. He senses my vulnerability and makes his move, sliding his hoof up the inside of my back legs and strumming my hairy harp. Without any guidance, he finds my wail switch and flicks it to 'on'.

My head spins. I feel helpless to stop him. He moves over me into some strange position like he's attempting some kind of farmer sutra. I can feel his baby's arm, hot and throbbing, and he's pushing it up against my bearded clam. But then I realise where I am and what's happening. I push him away.

"What you doing?" he asks abruptly.

"I'm getting up."

"Can't I meet Aunt Mary?"

"No." I push past him and head out into the glare of the day. And I don't look back.

Derek is away over the other side of the field, sniffing the air. I don't want him to see me.

So I head over to the water trough where Brenda is instead. My face still feels flush.

"You alright?" Brenda asks.

"YES! Jeez! I'm alright!" I say, lowering my head straight into the trough. The water is cool on my lips and I let it trickle down my throat. But I can't get that hot beaver cleaver out of my head.

That damned Tarquin.

***

It's later that night that I see Derek again. He comes to bed and starts picking the sheep shit off his hooves.

"Had a hell of a dump up the field just now." he says. "It looked like King Kong's finger. Could have flattened a car – it was that big. I looked like Louis Armstrong going for a top E trying to get that one out."

He lies down next to me and lets out a low growler.

"Sorry love. Had bad guts all day. Oof. Bit of a canary killer that one. Best hold your breath." he says, flinching backwards as the smell hits him in the face.

I sigh. I've never wanted him more.

"Your headache gone?"

"No."

My eyes are heavy and I start drifting into sleep.

Before I know it, Tarquin is stood proudly at the entrance to the barn - his shoulders, broad as the Tawe and his front legs brimming with pure muscle. Between his back legs dangle a glorious pair of clockweights. His fifth leg stands solidly to attention – rigid enough to hang a damp duffle coat on. It winks at me. My entire body tingles. I'm wanting to romance that bone oh yes. I lay back on the hay, and open my bomb doors for him. He looks at my spam fritters longingly and moves slowly but deliberately towards me. He knows what he wants and he's going to get it. My heartbeat quickens as I see his great love truncheon twitching like some huge dowsing rod approaching an area of great wetness.

"You got any Rennies love?" For a second or two, I try and figure out where I am and what's happening. Then the drab realisation hits home – I'm back in the barn.

And it's morning. And Derek's still in pain, clutching his guts.

"You alright?" I ask.

"No. It's that chilli I had last night. It's still fighting."

There's another low growl from Derek's arse – a smaller outbreak of chocolate thunder but still as intense as the one last night. It's dense and thick, hovering around the hay like some clammy Welsh mist. I can't take any more of this.

"Do you mind? I was having a lovely dream then. You've always got to go and spoil it haven't you?"

"Sorry. Not my fault." he says, grimacing and letting out another beef cloud.

I get up and head out into the field. I need the fresh air. It's a clean, spring morning and the wispy clouds drift lazily across the sky. I'd often dream of spending days like this in the field with the ram of my dreams. For a fleeting moment, I consider what I've ended up with – a weather-obsessed, loveless fartbag.

"Up early are we? Shat the bed?" I can tell

from the posh tones that it's Tarquin. He's back for more.

"Leave me alone Posh Boy." I say.

"Aw come on Dolly darling. I'm only having a laugh."

"Ha friggin' ha." I reply. He moves in behind me, brushing past my back door and sending goose bumps bouncing down my spine. If only Derek could have the same effect on me. I watch as Tarquin struts out over the field to a bunch of giggling girls.

Suddenly, I'm jealous.

I watch as he reduces the girls to quivering blobs of fluff. I recall what he told me the day before – about the girls in his old farm and I try to imagine it. Suddenly, I have the idea that could bring back the magic to my non-existent sex life with Derek. All I need is a camera and a willing friend.

3. A BREAK IN

"What say we make a film?" I say. My heart
has been bursting in anticipation of asking him.
Will he hate me? Will he love me? Will he think I'm
a slut?

"What? Like How Green Is My Valley?"
replies Derek, confused.

"No. More like Debbie Does Dallas."

Derek goes quiet. I fear I've overstepped
the mark.

"You mean you actually want to do 'it' with
me?"

"Yes. And on camera." Saying it out loud
makes my passion flaps quiver. Derek seems deep
in thought.

"Who'd film it?" he asks.

"Brenda - she's a Happy Shopper. I've already
spoken to her. She's in."

I hold my breath. Derek is showing no
emotion. But then a slow, wide smile spreads
across his woolly face.

"I love you." says Derek. He comes over
and gives me a big cwtch. It's been a long time
since he's had his sheepy arms around me. It feels
slightly strange – but nice – like it used to. Then he
suddenly gasps and pulls back.

"Where are we going to get a camera
from?"

"Farmer Honey has one – remember? The
one he takes to county shows."

Derek looks into my eyes. "You're a hell of

a girl."

"Yes. And I'm *your* girl." I reply.

***

It's Saturday morning and Farmer Honey and his wife have headed out to the local shops. Brenda's on standby to break into the farm house to get the camera.

"You know what the alarm signal is yes?" I say.

Brenda nods to herself. "Yes. Three bleats and I get my woolly arse out of there."

"Yes. And make sure you leave the place as you found it." I say, pulling the balaclava down over her face.

"You've pulled it down the wrong way Doll." says Brenda with muffled tones.

"So I have."

We laugh a nervous laugh as I turn the balaclava round and line the eye holes up with her eyes.

"All for a bit of rumpy pumpy eh?" she says.

"You'll enjoy it." I say. "Now go. We don't have long before the Honeys come back."

Brenda scarpers across the field and silently disappears behind the stone wall that surrounds the house.

Derek and I wait nervously from the safety of the barn. We keep our eyes glued to the road that leads up from the valley to the house, in case Farmer Honey's Land Rover should suddenly make an appearance.

"How long's she been gone now?" I ask impatiently.

"Erm…" Derek looks at the clock on the

barn wall. "Twenty seconds."

I sigh. It seems like forever.

Several minutes go by before there's a faint grunt down the valley.

"Oh no! They're back!" cries Derek.

I crane my neck to look. Sure enough, far down the valley, a Land Rover snakes its way up the side of the mountain.

"Quick! The alarm!"

"Baaaaah! Baaaaah! Baaaaaah!" calls Derek at the top of his voice. Our eyes fix on the house. Brenda has to get out. But there's no movement.

"Do it again!" I scream.

"Baaaaah! Baaaaah! Baaaaaah!"

Still nothing.

"Shit." The sound of the car's engine, grunting and spluttering up the hill is getting louder. And there's still no movement at the house. It's only a matter of seconds before the car pulls up.

"Baaaaah! Baaaaah! Baaaaaah!" Derek is desperate to be heard. But it's too late. Farmer Honey cuts the engine.

"He's going to go nuts with her if he finds her in the house. No-one has ever been caught in the house before." I mutter. Derek can do nothing but sigh and slump back against the barn wall.

I watch as Farmer and Mrs Honey get out of the car. They slam the car doors shut but just then, Brenda comes wandering around the side of the garden wall. I strain to hear the conversation. Farmer Honey doesn't seem too bothered and I watch him pat Brenda on the head and usher her away towards the barn.

She's not carrying a camera but as she trots on over, a sense of relief washes over me. I let out the breath I took in several minutes earlier.

"Did you get it?" I ask as Brenda steps into the barn.

"Of course I did." She leans back, lifts up one of her bellywarmers and pulls out the camera.

"I'm always grateful that I've got spaniel's ears for tits." she says. "Always comes in useful for stashing illicit goods and sundry items."

"Did you get a tape?" I ask.

Brenda's face drops.

"Bollocks. No. You never said…"

"We need a tape Brend."

"I found a cattle prod if that's any help!" she cries, lifting her other funbag and bringing out the prod.

"What the hell are we going to do with a cattle prod? We need tape!"

"Watch this!" Brenda takes the cattle prod and zaps Derek's arse cheek. He yelps and jumps two foot in the air.

"Alright! That's enough Brend!" I grab the camera from her and flick open the small screen. There's a small whirring noise as I turn the camera on and press 'Play'.

On the small screen flashes up some video footage of some sheep.

"What is it?" asks Brenda, peering over the top of the screen.

"The Royal Welsh Show. We'll tape over that. He won't miss it. Bloody sheep. They all look the same anyway."

"We can't keep the camera long. He'll notice." says Derek.

"I know. Looks like it's your lucky night then Weatherboy." I say.

4. LIGHTS. CAMERA. ACTION.

"Wiggle it in her face a little. I'm going round the back for a shot of the labial rashers Doll... ooh - your kipper could have done with a trim love. You've got yourself some thighbrows there. Careful now – don't bend over too far – you've got an eighteen spoker there love. Derek – move your conkers to the left – they're blocking my view of Dolly's clematis."

I'm laid out on a bale of hay in a private pen in the barn. Brenda's directing the action like she's done it before. It feels so liberating. Derek's stood over me, heaving his imperial barge into view and stroking it in a gentlemanly way in an attempt to get a yard on.

"Is there a draught in here somewhere?" Derek's concerned. "It's blowing right down my chocolate speedway and down over my thunderbirds."

"I can tell." says Brenda. "Your scrotum looks like Beadle's fist. Try and think about what you're about to do to your girl – on camera. That'll keep your pecker up."

"I can't keep it up. It's too damn cold in here."

"Yes you can. Focus. Ok. If you can just wiggle your towbar in front of the camera before you stick it in…that's it. Good lad. Don't worry about choreplay. Just take her straight up to your cannon wheels Derek."

Derek bears his woolly weight down on me. I'm about to be taken while Brenda records every second of sheep filth on film.

"Are you in yet?" I ask.

"Yes, you cheeky mare! Nearly up to my hairy love spuds."

Derek strains and forces his way in to my gammon flaps further and I feel his warmth inside me. He's really putting me to the sword, pinning me down and thrusting inside me like a big thrusting machine.

"Ok. Go for it Derek." calls Brenda, moving in to get a closer shot.

"Oh yeah. That's it." she says. "That looks just like the stuff they put on Channel 5." The more Brenda talks, the more turned on I get.

"Can I just say that you've got an awesome Judith." says Brenda.

"I know." I say, struggling to speak.

"Nice enough to turn me pie-curious actually." she says. "Might just have to growl at the badger myself you know." she whispers.

With that I feel another hoof on my foof. This is too much.

"I'm going to blow my stack." says Derek.

I look up at him, all sheep, taking what he wants from me, while I lay here helpless and at the mercy of him and Brenda.

"Mind if I take a wander through your lady garden?" asks Brenda. My whole body is wanting her to. Derek beats a hasty retreat to grab the camera while Brenda goes in to impersonate Stalin. Her hot tongue slip-slides all over my monkey's forehead. I grab the back of her head and grind her face down onto my Wirral peninsula.

"Film us Derek." I gasp.

"I am, I am!"

I can feel Brenda's bare hefferlumps

squashing against my legs as she reads the Financial Times. It's sending pulses of passion throughout my body and I close my eyes to savour the feeling. I open them to find Derek stood over me with his big, pounding thumper inches from my lips.

"You want to play my pink oboe?" he says.

***

The three of us lie flat out in the barn, looking up at the ceiling.

"Wow." I say. My entire body is still fizzing. I turn to Derek. He turns to me and smiles a weary smile. It's the first time in a long time that I've seen real happiness on his face.

"You're a great girl." he says. My heart flutters.

"You're not so bad yourself you know."

"Fair play Doll." pipes up Brenda. "If I had to choose between you two, I'd have to have you both."

"Hey - I haven't got a porn name." I muse.

"What about Debbie Grumble?" says Derek. I chuckle. "That's a nice name."

"And what will we call the film?" he asks.

"What about Debbie Does Dowlais?" says Brenda. We all let out a belly laugh before the barn falls silent as we rest.

"Yes. Debbie Does Dowlais. That has a certain ring to it, doesn't it?"

For a while, we lie there. I know that, like me, both Derek and Brenda will be running through what we've just done in their minds.

There's a sudden shuffle from across the barn. I look over and see Tarquin looking over.

"What are you peasants up to?" he snoots.

"Wouldn't you like to know?" I retort.

"What's that supposed to mean?" he asks.

"Let's just say that I'm a very lucky girl." I say, half-closing my eyes and letting out a deep, relaxing sigh. His face drops. It looks like he's just come in from a night down the pub with Morrissey. His miserable face is the last thing I see as I drift to sleep.

I wake up an hour later. In the darkness of the barn, I can feel the warmth of my man behind me and the woolly fuzziness of my sexy friend in front of me. For once, I feel totally satisfied. While the others sleep, I fancy a sneaky peek at the film. With my eyes half open, I pat my hoof around the hay for the camera.

Not there.

I open my eyes fully and jump up. My eyes dart around the hay around me.

"Shit! It's gone!"

5. A THREAT

Sheer panic grips me.
"Where is it?" I say. The other two grumble as they wake.
"Dez! Brenda! You got the camera?"
"No love."
"It'll be here somewhere. It has to be!" says Derek, rubbing his eyes. He's trying to keep me calm but it's not working. Not in the slightest.
I flip up the hay bales around me.
Nothing.
Derek gets up and goes scampering around the barn, waking some of the other girls nearby.
An hour later, we've found nothing and I'm in tears. I'm distraught. And I'm tired.
"It'll be around here somewhere." Brenda says.
I have nothing to say.

***

I don't sleep a wink. As a new day rises over the meadows, I head out and sit in the field in the watery morning sun. I want to be alone. Down near the barn, the flock wake and life goes on as normal. For me, it's the end of my world.
From behind the barn pops Tarquin's head. He looks my way. That's the last thing I want – Posh Boy trying it on. But I'm too late to avoid eye contact and he starts to saunter over to me. It seems like forever as he makes his way over. I don't

want to speak to him.

"What's the matter with you?" he asks.

"Leave me alone Tarquin."

"Charming!" he quips. "I thought you'd like to hear my good news."

"Not really." I can feel my face scrunch up.

"Well, I think you need to know – I've got myself my own small private barn, all to myself, so you won't be seeing too much of me during the nights anymore."

"Good." I say. "And why the hell do you get your own barn anyway?"

"Well, my former owner's very rich as you know." he says. I wish I hadn't asked. "He's paid Farmer Honey to have my own barn built so I can get some proper rest and privacy as I'm a very important sheep."

I cough up some phlegm and spit it out.

"Fine." he says and turns back for the barn.

"Oh. By the way. You been looking for something lately?"

"No. Nothing at all."

"Are you sure about that?" he sneers, his tone darkening.

"Yes. Now clear off. I don't want to speak to you."

"Oh, I think you may want to speak to me."

"No. No I don't. Not at all. Now please, piss off."

"Now now. You'll never get your camera back with that attitude Dolly."

"Tarquin – just…" The penny drops. My blood runs cold and drops to my hooves. I stand there for a second before I see red. I rush over to him and push my face right into his. I can smell last night's Pimms on his stupid sheep lips.

"How do you know about the camera?"

Tarquin pauses, enjoying the closeness.

"My. You have got beautiful eyes haven't you?" he says. I flip, pushing him down onto the floor and grabbing him by his throat.

"Where is my camera?"

"Mmm. This is nice. I do like a strongminded woman Dolly. Derek is a very lucky sheep." he witters.

"I'm giving you three seconds to tell me where my camera is." I demand.

"Alright, alright!" he says, relenting. I loosen my grip and he gets to his hooves, holding his throat.

"Wow. I must admit I did like that." he says.

"Where is my camera?"

"Oh, your camera's safe." he says. "For now at least."

My chest tightens.

"What do you mean?"

"Well, let's put it this way. I have something that you want and you have something that I want."

"What could you possibly want from me?"

I'm beginning to lose my control.

"Well let's say that I'm sure there's an agreement that we can come to." he says. "I hate to leave things unresolved." He paces around me, regaining his composure and casting glances at me.

"What do you want?" I ask.

"What do you think I want?" he says, disappearing behind me. I feel his lifeless eyes wandering over my dirtbox.

"Don't answer a question with a question." I say.

"Why?"

"Tsk."

"I'll be easy on you." he says. "I'll give you three choices." I don't want to hear them.

"One – you cough up £100 which you can nick from Farmer Honey's house so that I can decorate my new barn. A sheep like me needs his little luxuries."

Anger enflames me.

"He's a good man Farmer Honey. You leave him out of this." I snarl.

"Oh, he's nice enough, but if you can smuggle a camera out of the house, I'm sure you can get a few notes from the safe they have hidden in the wall there."

I sigh.

"Two – now this is my personal preference. Your second option is to make a movie like the one you've so splendidly done with Weatherboy and Bendy Brenda – but with me."

"Piss off."

"Oh dear." he says. "I'd say that was a lovely proposition seeing as we've got that chemistry going on between us."

"I'd rather stick pins in my eyes." I say. I'm not enjoying this one bit.

"Well you might have to do just that if you decide you'd rather the third option. You see, from my new place, I've got your camera set up to my laptop which itself is set up directly to the TV in the barn. Oh. And also to the world wide web. You know what that is right?"

"Don't patronise me Posh Boy."

"And what I'm thinking is that, should you decide not to take options one or two, I'd find it rather amusing to upload your splendid Debbie Does Dowlais movie to EweTube for the world to see. And not only that, but I can stream it straight to the TV in the barn while everyone sits down to watch The Apprentice."

My heart sinks. How could anyone be so cruel? He wouldn't do that surely?

"I'll leave you with those thoughts my love. I'll need to know by midday tomorrow." he says and wanders back down the field whistling, leaving me a broken sheep.

***

Lying alone in bed that night, I feel so alone. Derek's fast asleep next to me, snoring like a fog horn. But I can't sleep. Should I tell him? If I do, will he be angry with me? Is the £100 the easiest option? Brenda might be able to help. Aw, shit, she'll be angry too – she's caught up in all of this.

Decisions, decisions…

I feel a hoof sliding up the inside of my back leg. 'Not now Derek' I think to myself. He's half asleep but he's still got a bit of wind in his old boy. But I have to act normally. Quietly and slowly, I back up my coal hole to his soldier of love and within seconds he's up to his apricots in sheep.

As he nonchalantly pounds away at my peach half asleep, I come to my decision on what to do about Tarquin in the morning.

6. A DECISION

I take in a deep breath.

"I know who has our camera." I wait for the backlash.

"Who?" says Derek. I can't bring myself to utter Tarquin's stupid name.

"Who??" he asks again, growing impatient.

"Farmer Honey?"

"No."

"Juan the Lovesheep? It is, isn't it? That dirty Spanish…"

"No! It's not him…it's Tarquin."

"Tarquin?" he bellows. "What the hell's he doing with it?"

"He's…he's blackmailing us."

"For what? What does he want?"

I spend the next few minutes explaining it all in great detail. Brenda listens on intently. I feel very sad for Derek. He sits looking at the floor.

"My celebrity status as Wales's foremost weather forecasting sheep could be ruined. What will my Facebook and Twitter fans think? I know I like posting pictures of girls in wet T-shirts and pretending that they are rain deflectors an' all but they'll think that I'm a real pervert if this gets out."

I reach out my hoof and place it on his.

"We'll sort something out." I tell him reassuringly.

"I'll rip his balls off when I see him." says Brenda.

"We need to be careful Brend. If you go

ripping his balls off, he'll definitely want to get us back. We don't want him posting our video on EweTube. Derek's career will be in tatters."

"Well where are we going to get £100 from? I don't want to go stealing it off Farmer Honey." she replies.

"If we do 'borrow' if from Farmer Honey, we'll have to replace it. Maybe we could organise some kind of event to raise the money afterwards and replace it. But we need to decide quickly. Tarquin wants a decision by midday."

"Mmm." muses Derek. "That's a possibility. Maybe some kind of rodeo show or something."

"Well whatever. We'll pay it back with interest. We'll need you to go back into the house again Brenda. This could be the only way out."

"So you're not going to make a film with him then?"

"Like hell am I!" I say and look out over to the farm house to see the state of play.

"They're both in. And we need that money by midday. You're going to have sneak in while they're there."

***

It's another few tense minutes as Brenda slips into the farm house while Farmer Honey is away down the field on his tractor. She hides behind the stone wall until Mrs Honey pops out to put her washing on the line. I can't bear to watch but a few minutes later, Brenda appears in the doorway of the barn, panting.

I jump up.

"You get it?" I shout. Brenda nods a 'yes', too out of breath to speak. She's done it! All we need to do now is give Tarquin the £100 and get our camera back.

But within seconds, the large form of Farmer Honey stands behind Brenda in the doorway. And he doesn't look happy.

"I need to speak to you all right now." he says sternly.

***

Farmer Honey gathers the girls around him. We all fall silent as he prepares to speak.

"I've just got off the phone to Tarquin's owners." he says. "Over the last few months, Honey Farm has been losing a lot of money. I've been tempted to sell you off as a flock but you're my friends and I've held out from doing that for as long as I can. I've tried to protect you as much as I could, but now it's too much."

This sounds ominous. Farmer Honey continues.

"Tarquin's owners have offered us a lot of money for the farm. They've got a lot of cash and it's the only way out of the situation we're in. They're coming down tomorrow to sign the papers. I'm afraid that I'm going to have to sell you all on to other farms. I'm so sorry."

His bottom lip quivers.

"You mean we could be split up?" comes a voice from the back of the barn.

"That is a possibility yes. I'm sorry. Things are just really tough financially at the moment. I'm sorry."

And with that, Farmer Honey turns and heads back out to the farm house. He's visibly upset.

'Things just can't get any worse.' I think to myself. How wrong I am.

7. AN OFFER

"Oh come on in."

Derek, Brenda and I step into Tarquin's new barn. Opulent drapes adorn the walls and Tarquin sits reclining on a chaise longue with a glass of red wine. Over on the far side of his hay bed is a laptop, wired up to our camera.

Behind that is a luxury four-poster bed of hay.

It doesn't look good.

We step towards him.

"We've got the cash."

"Have you?" Tarquin puts down his wine glass on to a small table next to him and sits upright. He looks surprised. "Well, there's a shame." he says. "I was hoping that Dolly was going to serve up her cabbage for me."

"You ain't getting anywhere near my turnip." I say. "That's for Derek only."

"And Brenda of course."

"Yes." I say quietly. "And Brenda."

Tarquin reclines on the chaise longue again. "You see. I've always liked the idea of letting Percy in the playpen with some Welsh girls. I've had English of course. Bit boring though. Scottish girls were a bit wilder but they were always surrounded by midges for some reason. And as for the Irish…well, they were always nearly pretty, but never actually pretty. It's the Welsh girls I've always had a soft spot, or should we say, a hard spot for. Beautiful and passionate. Of course, being a single man, I have to rely on gentleman's periodicals to burp my worm. These days it's all becoming a case of hardbore rather than hardcore. I need real Welsh ewes to attend to my Spurt Reynolds."

"Well you're picking on the wrong girls here Posh Boy." says Derek. I know Derek's worried but he's trying his best to be brave.

"Oh shush it Romeo. You couldn't even get it up. Trying to knock a nail in with a plasticine hammer by the sounds of it."

"Well look." I say. "We've got the money so let's get this over and done with and let us have our camera back."

Tarquin picks off a grape from the bowl lying on the table next to him and pops it in his mouth.

"Where did you get the money from? Farmer Honey?"

"None of your business. We've got it here now and that's all that you need to know."

"It'd be a great shame to let him know that you've been in his house stealing money now wouldn't it?" he sneers.

Brenda moves forward. "I'll rip your balls off I swear." Tarquin gets up and lopes towards the laptop.

"Ah-ah. No you won't."

"Farmer Honey will ask why we stole the money if you tell him. Then he'll know your sordid little secrets." I counter.

Tarquin clasps his hooves together and puts them to his mouth. "Hm. Yes. You're right. Best keep Farmer Honey out of this. Don't want him going back on the deal with the farm and my owners now do we?"

Brenda lifts one of her fleshbombs and

takes out an envelope. Then she steps forward and throws it at Tarquin.

"There's your dirty money."

Tarquin takes his time to open the envelope and makes a point of sniffing the notes as he counts them.

"And our camera?" I demand.

Tarquin thinks.

"Do you know what? I've changed my mind." he says. "£100 is not enough. If you can get this lot as easily as you did, I'd like you to get me some more. I want £200."

There's a sudden twinge in my Bovril bullet hole.

Derek launches for Tarquin. Posh Boy moves swiftly to his laptop which sits opened on his desk.

"Woah! Not so fast Studmuffin. We don't want Debbie Does Dowlais to appear on the TV down at the barn now do we? It's all wired up ready to go look. All I need to do is click this little button here."

His hoof hovers over his laptop.

"You wouldn't dare." snarls Derek. I've never seen my man so angry.

"Oh is that right? All it takes is one tap on the keypad and whoompf - Derek's Uncle Fester is on EweTube for the whole world to see. Just one little touch…" he taunts.

"Okay, okay!" I shout. I have to put a stop to this. I take in a huge breath of air. "I'll do a film with you."

Derek looks at me crest-fallen. "You mean it?" he asks.

"I've got no choice Derek. He's got me by the spiders' legs." I notice tears welling up in Derek's eyes. I wink at him.

"You heard her Weatherboy. Now get out of my barn."

I turn to Tarquin. "I'll be back here at eight o'clock." I say.

Derek drops his head.

"Come on. Let's go."

"Good." he shouts back. "And bring Brenda." Tarquin calls after us as we leave.

"I look forward to making our cockumentary."

8. A FAREWELL

"You do realise that this will be the end of us if you go ahead with this?" says Derek. "I forgave you once with Juan in your last novelette of love, lust and sheep. But this will just be too much for me."

I take his hooves in mine.

"Baby, I don't have a choice in this. It's the only way I can get the camera back and save your career. I'm sorry. I have to do it."

The barn is quiet but we keep our voices low, not wanting to be heard.

"Why can't we just get another £100?"

"Brenda says that the £100 she got was the last £100 in the pot. We all know that Farmer Honey is broke. That's why he's put the farm up for sale. And besides, who's to say that dickhead won't up the price again?"

Derek sighs. I can tell he's heart-broken.

"What can we do about the farm being taken over by Tarquin's owners?" he asks.

For once, I don't know what to say.

"I don't know." I mutter. It's my admission of defeat. I don't know what else to say. I look around the barn. All the girls look sad and forlorn. This barn has been our home since we were born and to think that this could be one of our last nights here cripples me. And then I turn to Derek, my man. I cast my mind back to the day I first saw him here – the day I fell in love with him. Here we are now, at the end of it all.

"It doesn't have to be the end of us you know Derek." I say.

"I couldn't live with it." he says. He lays down and turns away from me.

"I was no good before this and I'm no good now." he mumbles.

I stand up and head over to Brenda, who's busy brushing her face, ready for filming.

"I'm so sorry that you've been dragged into all this." I say.

"Not your fault." she says. "Shit happens doesn't it? We're doing this for Derek."

"You've been a good friend Brend."

"I know."

"No, I mean it. We've had lots of fun over the years. I'm not sure what will happen to us once Tarquin's owners get hold of the farm but I just wanted you to know that you've been the best friend I've ever had."

Brenda turns to me.

"And you're the best friend I've ever had - in both meanings of the term." She smiles a half-smile before turning back to the mirror.

"Looks like we'll get one last bout of rugmunching in before we go our separate ways." she says.

"Apart from that bit, I'm not looking forward to it."

"Nope. Nor me. If I had my own way, I'd ruin that Posh Boy and not in a nice way." I smile at her but she doesn't see. She's still brushing her face in the mirror.

I head back to Derek, who's still lying on the hay. I want to hug him but I don't know what to say.

Brenda shuffles up behind me.

"We good to go?" she asks.

I sigh. "I guess so."

"Before we get there, I need to speak to you." she says. "I've been thinking. I've got a plan."

9. A TIE-UP

"Right. I'd like you both to tie me up and do what my other girls did to me." demands Tarquin.

Tarquin is laid out on the four-poster hay bed in his private barn, his love sausage stuck up in the air, waiting.

"Over there, you'll find some hoof-cuffs and a blind-fold."

I look onto the chaise longue where four sets of hoof-cuffs lie. I feel like I want to vomit. His laptop is sat on the desk, webcam pointed to the bed and ready to film the proceedings.

"Hurry up Dolly. I've been waiting all day." he says.

"You want me to tie you up like your other girls do you?" I ask.

"Indeed!" says Tarquin, laying back on his hay bed. I pick up the cuffs and blind-fold and head over to the bed. His battering ram, although large and throbbing, now makes me feel physically sick. In my mind's eye, it looks more like a pensioner's leg.

I lean over and attach his first hoof to the bed post with the cuffs. His eyes watch me.

"Can't wait to see your cunker." he says.

"Yeah?"

"Oh yes." His eyes wander over my grope fruits as I attach the other cuff to his second leg.

"Come and help her Brenda." he orders. Brenda steps out of the darkness and attaches the other two cuffs while I place a blindfold over his eyes.

Tarquin is now manacled to the bed.

But more than that, he's now totally at our mercy.

"You ready Posh Boy?" I ask.

"More than ready. Saturn V is ready for blast off! Take Captain Picard to warp speed if you will girls!"

I give a nod to Brenda. From under her spaniel's ear, she brings out the cattle prod she'd found at Farmer Honey's house and hands it to me.

"You tingling yet Posh Boy?"

"Ermm….nope."

"Okay…here we go."

I stretch out the cattle prod until it's millimetres from his quivering clems.

"Give it to me!" calls Tarquin.

"Oh I will."

With a zip and a snap, the cattle prod touches Tarquin's plums.

"JJJJJJJJJJJJJEEEEEEEEEEEEEZZZZZ! What the frig was that?" he yowls.

"What was what?"

"That…that…"

"You mean this?"

Zzzzzzpt!

Tarquin yells out once again. I move in close to him and whisper in his ear.

"Do you like that Posh Boy. Do you?"

His voice trembles.

"What are you doing to me?" he wails.

"It's called payback Tarquin. You want some more?"

"No! No! Stop!"

"Brenda – do the honours love will you?"

Brenda trots over to the laptop, disconnects Farmer Honey's camera and slips it under her shirt potato.

"Oh look. There's a webcam on this laptop." she says. She clicks a few buttons.

"Oh – and it feeds directly to the barn TV. Shall we provide that live link-up to the barn that you were on about so much Tarquin?"

"No!" Tarquin calls out. "No, please!"

Brenda presses a button and a small beep announces that the camera is live and broadcasting.

"Whoops." she says. "Already have." I move and stand in front of the laptop and address the girls who I know are now watching proceedings from the barn.

"Evening girls." In a small square in the corner of the screen, I can see scores of sheep eyes looking back at me. "Oh! I can see you all! Are you watching?"

From the laptop, I hear the mumbles of the girls down in the barn as they watch on with interest.

"I'm sorry to interrupt Emmerdale, but I've got a surprise for you! We've got here Tarquin. Most of you will know him as the toffee-nosed sheep on the farm." Brenda moves the laptop to line up the webcam with the stricken Tarquin laying shackled to the bed. I hear a sudden gasp from the girls down in the barn.

I continue. "Now that we're all here, Tarquin's got a few little confessions to make to you all."

"Undo these cuffs at once!" he cries.

"No chance." I say, moving closer. I lean right into him and speak directly into his ear.

"Now, tell the girls that you've been a naughty boy."

Tarquin grimaces. "No chance. This is

lesbianage. You won't get away with this. I'm a very rich…"

Zzzzzzzzzip!

"AARGH!"

"I asked you to tell the girls what you've been up to." I say.

"Never!"

Zzzzzzzzzzzip!

"Alright alright! Stop! Yes, yes! I admit it!"

Tarquin catches his breath. Then he announces meekily: "Yes, I've been blackmailing you!"

"Louder!"

"I've been blackmailing you!"

"Louder!"

"I'VE BEEN BLACKMAILING YOU!"

He begins to sob like a child.

"How?"

"I have a copy of your grumble flick and I've been demanding money from you."

Zzzzzzip!

"Argh! And Derek!"

Zzzzzip!

"And Brenda! Now please stop!"

On the screen, I see the girls, all stood and watching back. Right at the front of the crowd is Derek and beside him is Farmer Honey. I'm glad I told them to watch Emmerdale. The two lads have huge smiles smeared across their faces.

Back at the barn, Brenda and I arrive to a huge applause from the girls. Derek and Farmer Honey are there to greet us and Derek races to me, throwing his arms around me and giving me a big cwtch.

"I love you!" he says. Farmer Honey skips over and joins in the cwtch. "Thanks for giving us the heads up on this Doll." he says.

"I had a feeling that he was a rotten one but I couldn't quite put my finger on it. Thanks for bringing this to my attention."

"You can go get him if you want." I say. "We've left him tied up over there."

"No. I'm ok. I think we can leave him there overnight – keep him out of harm's way don't you think?" he replies.

∗∗∗

The following day, Tarquin's owners turn up to sign the papers. We watch as they disappear into the farm house, only to reemerge a few minutes later. They don't look too happy. As they flop into their car, Farmer Honey comes racing out, shouting after them.

"This farm is not up for sale! Keep your stinking money! And you can take your stinking sheep with you too!" he cries.

Later on, Derek, Brenda and I are snuggled up in the barn, reflecting on the day's events.

"A funny old day." I say.

"Ha. Yes. It was." says Derek. "But why didn't you tell me that you had a plan?" he asks.

"Because we didn't know if it was going to work. I didn't want you to worry."

"Well I'm very proud of you both." he says, wrapping his arms around us.

"Who fancies some action?" I say.

"Hey. Shall we watch our film while we're at it?" says Derek.

Brenda pulls out the camera and switches it on. There are a few beeps and for a few seconds, all we can hear is the bleating of sheep. Brenda stares at the camera.

"What's the matter Brend?"

She looks at the camera puzzled. "This is the Royal Welsh Show."

"What do you mean?"

"This is the Royal Welsh Show. This is what was on the tape before we made our film. I couldn't have pressed record."

FIFTEEN GRADES OF HAY:
GRAND SLAM

1. A PROPOSITION

"I've got a headache." I say.

"Again?"

"Yes."

"Aw no. You can't use that excuse again. You started the last book with that one."

"Well I'm not up for it this morning I'm sorry." Derek stands up.

"Brenda? You up for it?"

"I'm alright thanks Dez." she says, laying her head back down on the hay.

"Fine." Derek stands there for a few seconds, his lipstick swinging between his legs. "I'm going to buy a copy of the Wales on Sunday. They got the 50 Sexiest Sheep in there this week."

He slinks out of the barn and out into the cold. Brenda turns to me.

"You really have gone off nookie haven't you? You used to be up for it every morning."

I sigh. "Yes, but it's all a bit boring these days."

"But Derek is a weathersheep of international renown. Most sheep would give their right arms and legs to be mounted by him."

"Yes, but we're three books into the trilogy now. I feel it's dragged on far too much and there's not much to look forward to after this."

"Shut up mun." says Brenda. "We got the Six Nations starting this weekend."

"Aw no." I say. "That's the last thing I want. Bloody rugby." I lay my head on the hay and close my eyes. In my mind, I carry myself off to a hot beach, where I sip cocktails and feel the heat on my fleece.

***

It's a cold but bright morning down at the drinking trough. The chill morning mist lies draped over the fields, and low in the sky, a watery sun glows in a milky sky. It's a hint of spring.

"I've got myself a Wales top. I will put it for the games." announces Derek proudly.

"Saddo." I sigh.

What is it about rugby fans? They're almost as bad as football fans. All that singing, drinking and chanting. All to watch 30 men hammer the shit out of each other and then have a drink together after. I don't get it.

"So how did Wales do at the World Cup last year?" I ask knowingly.

"We got to the semi-finals."

"Then what happened?"

"We got our captain sent off in the first few minutes and then we missed an important kick to take us through to the finals."

"Typical." I say. "Chokers. Can't handle the real pressure can they?"

"Why do you hate rugby so much?" asks Brenda, dipping her face into the water trough.

"I used to watch it as a kid." I reply. "I'd get excited before each game and then we'd get smashed. It was like looking forward to Christmas each Saturday and then being told that you weren't getting any presents and that it had all been called off."

"I feel like that when I wake up every

morning with a raging lob on." says Derek.

"Well maybe I'll cave in and give you some lovings if Wales win." I say.

"They say that this is the best chance that Wales have got of a Grand Slam for years." says Derek.

"Yeah, well I reckon Wales won't be able to handle the pressure again. In fact, I'm so confident that the World Cup experience will get to them and they'll lose every game, I'm willing to give you some kind of action for every game that they actually do win."

"Oo. Now I'm listening." says Derek. "We've got Ireland up first. What will I get it we beat them?"

"Erm. A hoof job."

"Scotland?"

"Erm. A blowie."

"England?"

"You can take me properly if you beat them."

I throw caution to the wind. It'll never happen.

"Italy?"

"You can have me and Brenda together. Right Brend?"

Brenda nods "Aye. Count me in like."

"And if Wales win the Grand Slam?"

I stop and think. Grand Slam? I lean forward.

"I tell you what – if Wales win the Grand Slam, you can have a Grand Slam of your own." I say.

"What do you mean?" asks Derek, the corner of his mouth turning up in anticipation.

"You can have all the girls in the barn – all at once."

Derek's face lights up.

"All of them?"

"Yes. They won't mind. And I won't mind either."

"Why won't you mind? I'm your man."

"Because I know it'll never get that far!" I laugh. "Chokers, remember!"

I turn away and head down the field with my nose in the air. Outside, I'm certain that I won't even have to go anywhere near Derek's thunderrod.

But inside, there's a part of me that wonders if I've bitten off more than I can chew.

2. AN OLD FRIEND

"Hello Dolly."

It's a voice I recognise. I look up to see Juan the Lovesheep stood over me. I'll rephrase that: I look up to see Juan the Lovesheep's clockweights dangling down in front of my face. I quickly scramble to my hooves.

"What you doing in here?" I ask.

"It's a communal barn. I'm allowed in here."

"I know that stupid. I just haven't seen you down on the farm for ages."

"I've been keeping my head down lately. Derek is still probably mad at me after our little fling. How is the old bastard anyway?"

"He's fine ta. What do you want?"

"I've been thinking about you a lot lately. I just wanted to check that you are well."

"Well. Yes. I'm fine."

"I read about you and Tarquin in the last book. I bought it on Amazon."

"Yes. Well. The less said about him the better."

"I'm glad he never got his way with you. I can lay claim to the fact that I am the only one that you've strayed with."

"Get off your high horse Romeo."

"Well. Anyway. I was just wondering."

"Wondering what?" I ask.

"Whether you still think of me?"

"So you've come round here for a bit of an ego boost have you? Well, to answer your question, no, I don't think of you at all."

I glance at his strong Spanish shoulders and remember the time he touched my wail switch and took me to heaven.

"Why would I even think of you? You're history!"

My eyes wander over his flanks and down over his thick woolly thighs.

"Me and Derek are totally in love and that's all you need to know so you may as well head back out of that barn door and out of my life."

Juan looks at the floor.

"What you waiting for?" I say.

He turns and shuffles sadly out of the barn. It gives me a great excuse to clock the sack of potatoes that swing between his legs as he walks away.

***

The roar of a tractor engine shatters the tranquility of a cold but sunny Friday afternoon. From my position in the field, I see Farmer Honey trundling up the hill, pulling a trailer behind it. He pulls up in front of the barn and pulls up with a squeal. He hops down from the cab, walks around to the back of the trailer and drops the back end down.

"What's that Brend?"

"Beer."

From the bottom of the field, Derek trots over.

"Aw. He's good to us isn't he?"

"Yeah. He is that."

"Just been listening on the radio. They've been bigging up this Welsh team. I've got a feeling that my luck's in this year."

"Don't get ahead of yourself sunshine." I say.

"Wales haven't won anything yet."

"It'll be a different story this time tomorrow." says Derek and wanders over to the barn to cast an eye on the delivery of beer.

Brenda looks over to me.

"You really going to go through with this deal?"

"Hell yeah. Do you really think that Wales are going to get a third Grand Slam in eight years? They've got to beat Ireland in Dublin. Wales have won on just two of their previous six Dublin visits in the Six Nations, while Ireland can claim seven previous victories on the tournament's opening weekend for starters. Then there's England. Wales haven't won at Twickenham since 1998. Then there's France – we all know what happened there the last time we played them. Then of course, there's Scotland and Italy. Both of those can beat us on their day. So yes, I don't think we'll ever get to the point where Derek gets to sleep with the entire flock. Do you?"

"Fuggin hell. Someone's been cutting and pasting from Wikipedia. Talk about doom and gloom." says Brenda, rolling her eyes. "Don't think I'll even bother watching this year based on what you just rattled off."

"Yes. Well." I say. "We always start the year off thinking we can go all the way and it's a very rare thing."

Having convinced myself that Wales are in no danger of completing a Grand Slam, and that Derek isn't going to get his tool anywhere near the rest of the girls, I amble over to the barn to join the preparations for the Irish game tomorrow.

What I don't know is whether the boys in red are going to do what they did in 2005 and 2008 and go all the way.

A small part of me thinks they might. But only a small part.

3. IRELAND

The barn is buzzing. It's been like this since midday and the 3pm kick-off has kept Derek and the other girls waiting for three hours. They sit around the large TV screen on the barn wall, chattering and bleating. I stay away from the crowd, deciding instead to take myself off to a corner of the barn and read the latest Sweet Valley High book. This way, I can keep an eye on those Irish lads to make sure they do one over the Welsh - as much as I hate to say it.

"Girls, girls, girls!" Derek is stood on a hay bale at the front of the barn. What is he doing? The barn hushes to silence.

"Girls. Thank you…erm…I just wanted to say that as we kick off this year's Six Nations, that you could all be in for a treat should we go on to win the Grand Slam."

Oh no. Derek. Please don't mention our deal.

"Myself and my wonderful girl Dolly have made an agreement that should Wales go on to win all their games, that I get a Grand Slam of my own – and I get to give you all a good seeing to!"

The girls giggle and cheer with delight. They don't get much action. In fact, I can't see how they get any unless Juan manages to hang off the back of them one night when they're least expecting it. Derek cracks open a can of Skol and my heart sinks. What have I let myself in for?

Kick-off arrives. Penalty Ireland. I don't normally want Wales to lose but this is different and Ireland have got off to a good start.

Jonathan Davies scores in the corner. Silly sod. Just coming up to half time and Rory Best, Irish hooker goes over for Ireland. If their hooker can go over, that should send alarm bells ringing for Wales. I can see where this one is going and I close my eyes and drift off to sleep.

Twenty minutes later, I'm woken by a roar from the girls. I sit up and look at the replay. Big George North thunders through a handful of Irishmen and sends Davies over for another one. Halfpenny slots the conversion and Wales take the lead.

Bollocks.

I move around to join the girls in front of the TV. Another Ireland penalty. They take the lead. Thirteen minutes to go. Ireland lay siege to the Welsh lines, hurling themselves at the Welsh players. Come on Ireland. You can do it. Merciless, unstoppable, they keep coming but somehow the Welsh hold out. They have to buckle, they have to. The ball goes wide, where the red line is thinner and Tommy Bowe slides in at the corner. Had to be an Osprey didn't it?

Ireland 21 Wales 15.

Wales have no chance. I smirk to myself.

Derek won't even be getting a hoof job at this rate. Hoo-fricking-rah.

Then Big George steps up, blasting his way through several Irish players, crashing through the Irish line and taking the ball with him.

Ireland 21 Wales 20. I start to sweat.

Halfpenny lines up to kick the conversion in the last four minutes. He has to miss. He has to. And he does. I skip gleefully out into the sunshine outside singing to myself. I head down to the bottom of the field where the grass is juicier and have a munch. Nom nom nom.

A few minutes later, there comes a distant shriek of sheep from across the field. I stop chewing and listen.

Nothing. Just the whisper of the wind, tumbling across the field. Then a collective howl from the barn. Something's happened.

A few seconds later, Derek comes Irish jigging out of the barn. He hasn't noticed me down the bottom of the field and he is soon surrounded by the girls who spill out of the barn.

"Hm." I think to myself. "This doesn't look good."

***

An hour later, Derek is laid out on our hay like he's waiting to go down Whiteface Mountain on a luge.

I sigh. Bloody Leigh Halfpenny and his stupid boot. I reach out my hoof and touch Derek's pud. It instantly stands to attention.

"Up periscope." I say and start polishing his genie lamp.

"You're so good." he says.

"I know." I say, looking around the barn and wondering whether it needs a lick of paint around the place.

"Show me your udders." he says. "I want to see your fleshbombs."

"Just hurry up will you? I'm getting cramp."

"Give me some filth pillow talk." he says.

"Erm…"

"Call me names!"

"You erm….big hairy sheep."

"YES!"

"Erm…you slag."

"OH! That's it! Keep going!"

"Erm…you big woolly…erm…slag."

Derek arches his back, his face contorted. He looks like Hendrix on the high notes. The ends of his hooves curl up like jester's shoes as he blows his stack. A small dollop lands on the end of my nose.

"Oh baby!" he calls out.

"Got a tissue?" I ask.

4. SCOTLAND

With Ireland kicked into touch, I don't hold out much hope of Scotland beating Wales, especially at home. I resign myself to the fact that I may have to go through with the next promise I gave Derek.

The barn is busy once again as the girls and Derek take their places to watch the Scotland game. One of the Shetland ponies has come in to watch the game but is forced by the Welsh girls to sit at the back next to me.

I stay in the background, watching the TV from the back of the barn. After 25 minutes, Scotland take the lead with a penalty. And 3-3 at half time. I don't want to get too smug. Not yet.

Second half starts and the huge frame of Alex Cuthbert rampages over for a try. How can I not celebrate Wales scoring? A few minutes later, Wales score again through Leigh Halfpenny. He's short, but cute. Then I watch as he lines up for the kick. His arms are huge – he can move mountains with them. The sight of them sends a tingle to passion flaps. Maybe I'm enjoying this rugby too much.

I have to control myself. I still have to give Derek his fun should we win. But I want us to score again, just to ogle Leigh Halfpenny's arms. I'm torn.

My fate is sealed a few minutes later when my little man goes over again for another try. I feel my bilge tanks stirring as he lines up another kick and find myself dribbling at the TV screen.

"You ok?" asks the Shetland.

I don't answer.

***

A few hours later, and Derek is back on the hay, Soldier Of Love stood to attention, awaiting his horatio. Wales have another win.

I sigh.

"You've got England up next. At HQ. Your fun stops here Derek the Weathersheep." I say.

"Yes, yes. Whatever." he says. "Now get your gums around these plums."

Reluctantly, I lower my head and take his Cyclops into my mouth. Strangely, since my perv at Leigh Halfpenny's arms, I'm more in the mood than I think. Taking it all in like some kind of pink sword swallower, I neck his throbbing podge-on like some hungry gannet. He moans, his truncheon throbbing in my gob. He's hard. Harder than Chinese algebra.

I keep going at his pink steel, relentless, merciless, until finally, and without warning, he explodes like a Buncefield oil terminal.

Derek lies there flat out as I head back into the barn to find my bottle of Listerine.

5. TAKING STOCK

After the last two games, I'm seriously beginning to worry about my bet. I'm relaxing in the spring sunshine when Juan the Lovesheep wanders over again. Does he ever give up?

"Morning." he says.

"Correct." I reply.

"I had a dream about you last night. I thought you should know."

"That's nice." I say.

"Yes. It was just me and you, making mad passionate love on a beach in Barrybados."

"Nice. I bet I was good."

"Oh yes. You were."

I'm intrigued. I often wonder what others think of me in the quiet of the night.

"You took me to heaven and back right there on the shoreline. And then we went to Just Pennies amusement arcade and we won 50p on the slot machines."

'Right now I wouldn't mind him having a go on my slot machine.' I think to myself. 'He'd really hit the jackpot'.

"And then after that, we came back to Honey Farm…" he continues.

"Yes, alright I get the picture!" I snap. "Well it ain't going to happen lover." I tell him, despite my body craving for every inch of his woolly frame.

"And that's final."

Juan looks sad. I know he tries it on with

most girls on the farm but I do think back to the times we spent together. And in the warm glow of the spring sunshine, it all seems so good.

That idyll is shattered by Brenda's booming voice.

"What's Donkey Dick doing here?" she bellows. I spin around to see Brenda ambling up to us.

"We're just catching up." I say.

"I was just leaving." says Juan before quickly trotting off across the field.

"Damn right you are." says Brenda after him. She turns to me.

"You're not going back there are you?" she asks.

"Don't be silly." I reply. "I've got more than my hands full with that silly bet I put on with Derek. I'm worried that Wales will win every game and I'm going to have to let him get jiggy with every other girl in the barn."

"Why don't you call it off?"

"I can't do that. You can't go calling bets off halfway through just because it looks like you're going to end up on your arse. I'm just going to have to grin and bear it if I do lose."

"I wouldn't worry too much – it's England tomorrow and they're at home. Wales have about as much chance as winning that as I have becoming the next Prime Minister of Bolivia. I think England will trample all over them. They've been unstoppable so far."

"Let's hope so." I say.

6. ENGLAND

I'm facing a dilemma. England v Wales. I'm a Welsh girl through and through. Every fibre of my woolly fleece screams Cymru. But I'm also a competitive girl. I don't want Derek to go winning his bet.

When I arrive at the barn, Derek's already there. He's got himself a front row seat with a beer in his hand – he knows that a win over the Saes will mean he gets to give me a good pounding. Is a Welsh win worth gritting my teeth and bearing it?

Mae Hen Wlad is bellowed out by those in the barn. I'm pretending to watch the game out of interest for the sport but really I'm there to see Leigh Halfpenny's arms.

And there he is! My leisure trove fizzes and I have to readjust my seating arrangements. But within minutes, he's absolutely clattered attempting to catch a high ball. I jump up, my heart in my mouth. How dare they flatten my man!

Derek looks over to me. I suddenly catch myself and quietly take my seat with a squelch.

Twenty minutes in and England pull ahead through a penalty, yet five minutes later, Halfpenny brings the game level to 3-3.

England nick ahead again – another penalty. Farrell kicks ahead, catching the ball and steaming towards the Welsh line until he's smashed back into the ground with a sickening thud by Big George North. Have that you English…again, I stop myself. This could be serious. But England pile on the pressure, and take a 9-6 lead at half-time.

Phew.

I trot over to grab a beer. Derek's there, chatting to some of the girls. They suddenly stop talking when I arrive.

"You ok Doll?"

"Yes, thank you." I say, yanking a beer from the case.

"Do you think Wales will stage a late comeback like they always do?" he asks. I look the two girls he's with up and down. They both look at me with their slutty sheep eyes.

"What you looking at?" I say.

The two scrubbers turn to each other and slink off back to their seats.

"You'd really do them?" I ask.

"You said I could!"

"I said you could if Wales won all their games. We're only half way through and Wales are losing." I turn and head back to my seat.

The game resumes and England stretch their lead. 12-6. Double figures always feels good. Priestland gets sent off. I'm beginning to feel more comfortable. Then Wales hit a penalty. The game drags on until, with just 10 minutes left, Wales strike another penalty.

12-12.

That's probably the perfect way to end the game. Wales don't lose, but they also don't win the Triple Crown and potentially the Grand Slam. And Derek can't get his end away with a barn full of fuglies.

Seven minutes to go.

Six.

Five.

So that's it. A draw. England come again

with a turnover from Halfpenny. I can see what's going to happen. Same old story. I'm just waiting for Gareth Charles to mention 'desperate defence from Wales' and then a sneaky try from a toff Englishman who's just come on.

But no.

Something happens. Something incredible. And for me, it all happens in slow motion. The Welsh line, still reeling from the English onslaught, hold firm. Strong Welsh arms rip the ball from the Saes, and the ball is popped upfield. A red jersey goes streaking after it, slicing through the white line. The ball bounces in the air – it's all in the timing.

The ball lands safely in the Welshman's arms. He goes charging ahead. An Englishman leaps in from the side. I can't watch. But I do. The Welshman charges on, punches the air, leaps over the line and comes down with a crash.

Wales are ahead.

My legs start shaking. We're beating England. At Twickenham. We're on for a Triple Crown. That means that we're also on for a Grand Slam.

Aw bollocks.

***

Half hour later, I'm bent over the fence down the bottom of the field being shafted by Derek.

"Now that's what I call a game!" he says, gripping my hips with one hand and swigging at his Skol from a can in the other.

"Just concentrate on what you're doing." I say, pushing back my peach to get more of his pink hoe inside me. He finishes his beer and tosses the can away, bringing his two hooves around to grab my Zeppelins and pound me hard.

"And I think Italy will be a walkover but I must admit that I am a little concerned about France."

"Well let's hope that France stuff us like you're stuffing me right now. I don't want your todger being shared all over the farm."

7. ITALY

Sigh.

There's no stopping the Welsh boys now. Italy at home. I don't even bother watching this one. Instead, I take myself down to the bottom of the field. Not only are Wales getting the results they want, but so is Derek.

I lie on my back and take in a large gulp of spring air. I start thinking about how I'd feel if Wales win the Grand Slam. Will I really be able to handle my man sticking his dipstick in all those other girls? I thought I could handle it. Now I'm having second thoughts. But I can't go back on my word. We made a deal. And I have had my fair share of fun in the past. As I lie there, I drift off, into another place where sheep are lusting over me. I lay back, gazing up at the rams stood over me. They all want me. Their yellow eyes wander longingly all over my woolly bits.

"Now there's a nice bit of tosstalgia for you." comes a voice. "An arse like a jazz trumpeter's cheeks and a vertical smile that warms and ram's heart."

Sigh.

"Juan – you never give up do you?"

"I long for your kangaroo pouch."

"Ey – we don't play the Wallabies until the summer."

He moves towards me. I holds my shoulders and presses down. I feel his manly strength forcing me down.

"What the frig is going on??" It's Derek – here to ruin my moment.

"I was just asking her to…"

Derek stomps over and pushes us apart.

"I thought you were finished with him."

"I…I…" I can't think of anything to say.

"Come on – you're coming with me to watch the boys do one over Italy." He grabs me and drags me into the barn like a rag doll.

Inside, the girls are already merry, whooping and hollering as John 'Let's Talk About England' Inverdale appears on the screen.

I can see what's coming. Another Welsh win and I'm in the haysack with Derek and Brenda. Wales leave it late to show their superiority but win they do and two hours later, I'm on my back awaiting a good pounding. Brenda's lying by my side.

"Get this choreplay over with quickly Brenda." I whisper to her "I can't stand all this frigmarole of pretending to enjoy girl-on-girl just for him."

Brenda crouches down, growls at the badger and goes truffle hunting. Derek watches from a short distance away, touching his lad. Don't get me wrong, Brenda's a lovely girl but she does look like she goes jogging behind gritter lorries. I close my eyes and think of Juan. I imagine his sheepy lips flitting over my blit.

"Sit on her face." orders Derek.

"We're not playing guess her weight Derek." I reply.

"Do it." he barks. Brenda moves up and squats over me, her clopper just inches from my face.

I sigh. Me and my stupid bet.

8. GRAND SLAM

Ok. This is it.

There's a minute's silence for the great Merv the Swerve at the stadium. As the nation reflects, it's the calm before the storm.

"It's not going to be pretty. It's going to be brutal." says Jonathan Davies, trying hard not to refer to 'inside shoulder' or 'numbers'.

Within the first minute, Lionel Beauxis tries a drop goal which skims the soft surface of the Millennium Stadium. Hm. They look nervous. But within ten minutes, they're ahead thanks to a penalty.

Then Wales get their chance. Priestland boots it, thumping the post and missing a chance to level. Not sure why my lad Halfpenny wasn't given a chance. Five minutes later, Lydiate scythes down Dusautoir, stealing the ball and getting it wide to Cuthbert. He puts his head down, switches on the afterburners and throttles for the line.

He's over.

The crowd at the Millennium Stadium go wild. Halfpenny thumps over the conversion. Wales are on their way.

More Welsh pressure and the French are beginning to buckle. Another Welsh penalty takes the score to 10-3 and on the stroke of half time, there's another, Halfpenny bouncing it off the sticks again.

Phew.

But then news comes through that Sam

Warburton won't be reappearing. That's three times now in this Six Nations that he's gone off injured. It seems he's destined not to finish a game against the French.

We head into the second half. This is possibly the biggest 40 minutes that these players will face for a few years. Taking it all in, I will the 15 boys in red to nail it, despite the outcome of my deal with Derek. This opportunity doesn't come around very often.

The French start the second half with some vigour, pulling back a penalty and a few minutes later, catching Cuthbert in the bollocks. The clock is stopped for some treatment to his plums. The way I'm feeling, I'd kiss them better myself.

Despite the French power, Wales win a penalty on the halfway line, Halfpenny drilling the ball far downfield and through the uprights. But France come back harder and stronger. They're not going away and set up camp in the Welsh half. Bodies litter the field as France bludgeon the Welsh. And with seven minutes on the clock, the French win a penalty. They decide to kick, bringing the score to 13-9.

My anus starts twitching.

And then Wales fight back. My man Halfpenny makes a break, very nearly getting through, but it takes two Frenchmen to drag him to the ground. The momentum swings, now favouring the Welsh. The pressure tells when with five minutes left on the clock, Halfpenny thuds over another penalty.

For the last five minutes, the clock in the corner of the screen seems to run in slow motion. Priestland tries a drop goal but the advantage is now with Wales. And five minutes later, Wales are

Grand Slam champions.

The barn erupts. There are sheep bouncing all over the place, beer splashing up on the air and happy faces all around. I dive into the crowd, helpless to resist the delirium.

"We've done it!" cries Brenda. "We've done it!"

The barn door flies open. There, with a large magnum of champagne in his grubby hands is Farmer Honey. There's a 'pop' as the cork shoots over our heads and Farmer Honey raises the bottle high in the air.

"Who bloody wants some?" he calls out.

***

As the celebrations continue, I head outside to clear my head. The cool fresh air slaps me around the face and I suck in a lungful. Then I realise what that means for Derek. Before I have time to think, a shadow looms to the right of me.

"Ah. We meet again." I turn to see Juan the Lovesheep stood gazing at me.

"Hello Juan. Yes. We meet again."

"Where is your fellow?" he asks in his Spanish tones.

"I don't know to be honest. Probably off his tits somewhere."

"You look concerned my friend." says Juan.

"Oh it's nothing." I reply.

Juan tilts his head to one side and pouts his bottom lip.

"Oh, it's Derek. Me and him made some silly deal. Just means he's going to give his love truncheon to every girl in there now that Wales won the Grand Slam."

"What's wrong with that? That's what us men sheep do. If we were on a David Attenborough show, viewers would think that we were right slags. But that's just the way we are."

"Well maybe but I like to think that Derek and I have something special."

"You weren't saying that when you helping yourself to a portion of my cheesecake."

"That was ages ago. When I was young and vulnerable."

"Life is too short. You were just enjoying yourself, as I'm sure Derek will later. He'll still love you. In fact, he will probably love you more for it."

There's a sudden crunch as the barn door falls open and Derek falls out face first onto the gravel.

"Derek!" I lurch forward and crouch down to check him.

"Derek! Are you ok?" I lean my head in to his.

"I...I...I'm nissed as a pewt." he mumbles into the ground. I look up at Juan who shrugs his shoulders. "I'm wanning my Grand Slam." he slurs.

Juan looks at me before ducking out and heading out across the field. Derek raises his weary head.

"Oh my God." he says "Just look at you all there. Right. Whooo's first?" He tries to smile and his eyes are all over the place. I look behind me.

There's no-one there. But Derek thinks otherwise.

The drink has obviously affected his vision.

"I'd like to take you aaaaall at once." he says, moving forward. "I'll 'ave er...you...you there. I'll have you there first."

I step forward, Derek raising his hoof to my

face. He touches it.

"You're so beautiful you know. Much more so than Dolly."

He's really off his face. His eyes wander all over the place.

"Oo. And look at you." he says. "Can I do you please?"

The more I look at Derek, the more I realise how drunk he is. And the more I realise that I could actually get away with not letting him get his hooves on the other girls. He's so off his tits, he can see more than one of me and he actually thinks he's with a group of sheep. He actually thinks he's having his Grand Slam.

"Come on Derek – let's get down to action." I say, helping Derek as he stumbles down towards the barn. Out of the corner of my eye, I spot a face peering around the corner of the building.

It's Juan.

I wink at him.

"Fancy joining us?" I say.

———

ABOUT THE AUTHOR

Derek The Weathersheep lives on a Rex Honey's Farm high in the Brecon Beacons, South Wales.

From his high vantage point, Derek can cast his sheep's eye across the whole of South Wales, and forecast the South Walian population about forthcoming
weather events.

He first caught the meteorological bug when he was just a lamb. He was the first sheep to correctly forecast the great snows of 2006, when he ran to Farmer Honey's house, woke him from his slumber, bleated for a bit, and then led Farmer Honey to the rest of the sheep who were about to be cut off from the farm by the drifts. 48 sheep were rescued that night. Farmer Honey rewarded him by presenting him with the Freedom of Honey Farm.

Derek's girlfriend, Dolly (not to be confused with the famous cloned one- they just look alike) is the best looking ewe on the field, and constantly draws attention from male sheep and sometimes even other female sheep. Juan the LoveSheep, a Spanish import, brought by Farmer Honey, to increase virility in the flock, constantly tries to woo Dolly, much to Derek's dismay and amusement.

Also available:

- Fifteen Grades of Hay
- Fifteen Grades of Hay: The Sex Tape
- A Woolly Yarn: The Derek the Weathersheep
Autobiography
- A Winter's Tail

Details at www.weathersheep.com